After an extremely interesting nursing career, the author is now very happily retired. In the last 20 years she has experienced many adventure holidays: cycling safaris in Kenya and Tanzania, she climbed Kilimanjaro, trekked in the Himalaya, the Atlas Mountains, the Peruvian Andes, the Transylvanian Alps and the Wall of China.

In 2002 she won first prize in her 1932 Austin Ten (Gypsy) doing Lands End to John o'Groats for Christian Aid.

She presents public slide shows about her travels, is involved in church activities, plays 'cello in a local orchestra and enjoys gardening and her cats.

WEATHER PERMITTING

Anne Mosscrop

WEATHER PERMITTING

AUSTIN & MACAULEY

A CIP catalogue record for this title is available from the British Library.

ISBN 978 1 905609 89 5

www.austinmacauley.com

First Published (2009)
Austin & Macauley Publishers Ltd.
25 Canada Square
Canary Wharf
London
E14 5LB

Printed & Bound in Great Britain

DEDICATION

To Claire, who first invited me to Canada

ACKNOWLEDGEMENTS

Thank you to all those who gave me helpful and constructive comments on the manuscript: Fiona Bennett, Judith and Michael Littleboy, Mary Curtis, Christine and George Bell, Maddie and John Clark, Lydia Bishop, Kathleen Slade, Hilary and Mike Baker and Holly Chapman. A big thank you to Fiona Bennett, Brian Hesketh and Michael Littleboy for their patience coming to my aid with computer skills, especially Michael's clever work on the maps.

Maps: © Collins Bartholomew Ltd Reproduced on 1961 Readers Digest World Atlas by kind permission of Harper Collins Publishers
www.collinsbartholomew.com

CONTENTS

PROLOGUE   15

INTRODUCTION   17

FOREWORD   23

CHAPTER 1 FORT CHIMO   25

CHAPTER 2 GEORGE RIVER   53

CHAPTER 3 GREAT WHALE RIVER   86

CHAPTER 4 IVUJIVIK   95

CHAPTER 5 SUGLUK   100

CHAPTER 6 MY PARENTS' VISIT   135

CHAPTER 7 CHICKENPOX INTERLUDE   150

CHAPTER 8 SUGLUK 1970 (continued)   155

CHAPTER 9 POVUNGNITUK AND GREAT WHALE RIVER
1970   164

PART TWO 1971   171

CHAPTER 10 GREAT WHALE RIVER 1971   173

CHAPTER 11 GREAT WHALE RIVER 1972   178

CHAPTER 12 TB INTERLUDE   193

CHAPTER 13 FORT GEORGE   204

CHAPTER 14 FORT GEORGE AND RUPERT'S HOUSE 1974
216

EPILOGUE   227

PROLOGUE

May 7th 1970

"The storm has been raging all day, the worst we have ever had. Father Verspeek reckoned that the wind was about a hundred miles an hour. He came in for a little while this afternoon, to sit with mother and baby so that Susie (who has now taken over from Mary as my interpreter) and I could go out and visit the two patients. Just before we went out Father Verspeek told us about two girls in POV who walked through their village in a similar storm and not being able to see where they were, probably thought they were lost and carried on past the village. They were found dead of exposure the next day, not far from home. A cautionary tale. Susie and I could hardly see where we were going in the blizzard and we made our way through the village on our hands and knees, hanging on to each other as we went. Once again I was reminded of Scott's expeditions. Kalingo's condition was still stable, I just pray that he can hold on and his appendix won't rupture. Josephie's finger was comfortable so that was a relief. It is now 6 p.m. and I am once again playing the waiting game..."

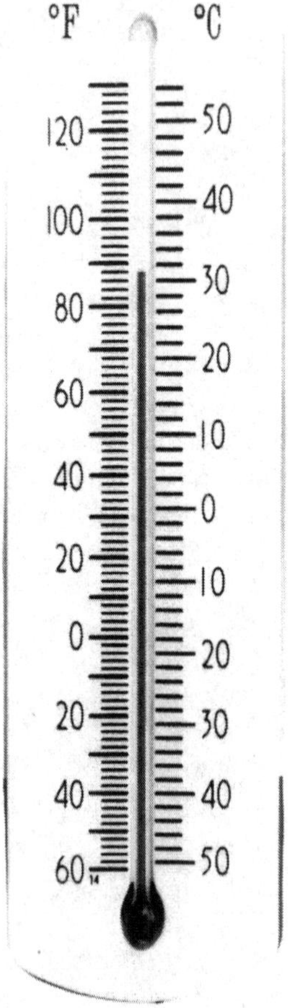
°F
°C
120
100
80
60
40
20
0
20
40
60
50
40
30
20
10
0
10
20
30
40
50

INTRODUCTION

A group of us sat in the sixth form common room discussing what we would be doing in ten years' time. One girl already had her eye on her future husband who was twelve years older than her and I believe, she did actually marry him. As for me, I was sure to be married (nobody as yet lined up) and would have at least four children by then. Little did I imagine that I would be working in Denmark, the country where I first learned about Eskimos and where my life was about to change dramatically.

I was born in 1939, the oldest of three 'war babies'. My mother rented two rooms on a farm during the war while my father was away in the Air Force. Like many mothers at that time she was virtually a single parent but we were fortunate in that my father (unlike many) did come home after the war. He was guaranteed his job as chief cashier in a Lincoln bank, which he took up again on his return. He hated being indoors and spent his time longing to be working outdoors. He left the bank in 1950 and with my mother, who was qualified in poultry management, started a poultry farm where I also helped out during school holidays. After leaving school my first job was looking after sheep on a nearby farm. I then spent three months in Ireland as a governess to two young boys, one of whom had Downs Syndrome, while waiting to start my nurse training. I qualified in general nursing and psychiatric nursing before going to Switzerland in 1964 where I worked in a hospital in Lausanne for two years. I was already bilingual before going to Switzerland, having been to France several times while still at school. After my time in Switzerland I arranged to go to Denmark and work in a hospital in Århus. I met Claire, my French Canadian friend, in

Lausanne before I went to Denmark and she persuaded me to spend a year in Montreal with her when I returned from Denmark. In 1966 I went to Denmark and it was there I first learned about Greenland Eskimos from Danish nurses. I was fascinated and decided that after my year in Montreal I would return to Denmark and be seconded to Greenland. I spent 16 months in Denmark and quickly learned Danish. I left for Montreal in 1968 after a six month spell in Scotland doing the Part 1 midwifery course which was a prerequisite qualification for entry into Quebec. I sailed to Montreal on the Empress of Canada, which at that time was the cheapest way to travel. The journey across the Atlantic took a week.

After only a few months in a large Montreal hospital I was utterly bored. As a qualified nurse with several years of experience, my work there was mainly office work while the nursing care was carried out by nursing assistants. I was not ready to be pen-pushing. As I could not afford to return to Europe (it had taken me a year to save up for the fare) and I felt I wanted to see more of Canada, I wrote to the Quebec provincial government to ask if they had any jobs working among the Eskimos. I was offered a job immediately. I decided that it would be interesting to spend a year in the Canadian Arctic before going to Greenland and to compare the two experiences.

As it happened I never got to Greenland; I spent over four years in the Canadian Arctic.

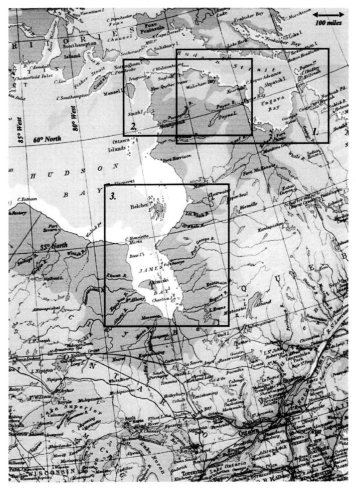

Eastern Canada and Hudson Bay

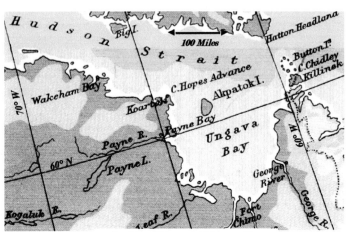

1. Fort Chimo and Ungava Bay

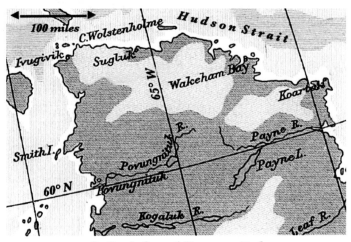

2. Sugluk and Povungnituk

3. James Bay

FOREWORD

I have had several attempts at writing this book over the years but now (2005) have decided to write directly from my letters to my parents, which doubled as diaries, with a few additions of things I didn't tell them at the time and some general 'tidying up'. To my delight, in 2003 I came across a diary written by my father in 1970 when my parents stayed with me in Sugluk that year. I had no idea he had written this and as I obviously did not write to my parents during those three weeks, his diary fills that gap so I am including it in my book.

Today it is politically correct to call Eskimos the 'Inuit' but as I am writing from my letters which were written between 1969 and 1974, I would like to keep to the language of the day. I don't know if Cree Indians are called anything else today. For the same reason, all temperatures I mention are in degrees Fahrenheit. I hope the reader will find the comparison chart with degrees Centigrade useful.

I learned quite a lot of Inuktituk and soon understood that 'inuit' simply meant 'the people', 'inuk' meant 'a person' and 'inuktituk' 'language', i.e. their language. Originally they did not know of any other kind of people than themselves. When the white man came on the scene, they had to find a word to differentiate and the white man became 'kadluna', (kabluna or kapluna, depending on the dialect).

The two common questions that people ask me are, "How did you end up in the Arctic?" and "Where did your sense of adventure come from?" The first is easy to answer as I have outlined above. The second is not easy to answer. I have put a great deal of thought into trying to answer other than "I don't know," and have come to the conclusion, with apologies to Shakespeare, that "Some people are born adventurous, some achieve adventure and some have adventure thrust upon them." In my case, maybe a mixture of all three. With my gift for languages I have enjoyed being able to work in a few different countries, thus combining work, languages and travel.

CHAPTER 1
FORT CHIMO

February 1st 1969

Having been fascinated by the Arctic for some time I am thrilled
to have been offered a job with the Quebec provincial
government, outpost nursing among the Eskimos in the Arctic. I
am very excited and can't wait for the interview next week when
I shall find out all about this new work. Then, next year, as I plan
to go to Greenland, it will be interesting to compare the two
experiences.

February 6th 1969

Yesterday I went to Quebec City for an interview at the
provincial government headquarters, itching to find out about
my new work, something totally unlike anything I have done
before. Madame B, the supervisor, was very charming and put
me at my ease. She gave me the impression she was relieved to
find someone actually wanting to work in the Arctic. I had
requested to go to a small village where Eskimos are still living in
primitive conditions, away from civilisation. She told me my luck
was in as there is a post in a little village which is vacant at the
moment. She pointed it out on the map, right on the tip of
Ungava Bay and Labrador. In the excitement of the moment I
forgot to ask its name and she omitted to tell me but I looked it
up later. It is called Killinik. I will have to spend a few weeks
working at the hospital in Fort Chimo and have some training

from the doctor there, in order to get into Killinik before the break-up starts in May. Madame B wants me to leave on the 4th March in order to fit in this training before the break-up. Fort Chimo is the headquarters of the various little settlements in the Ungava Bay area and everything is organised from there. The only doctor is based at the hospital in Fort Chimo. Most of my orientation will involve working on the wards, the outpatient clinic, home visiting, examining schoolchildren, immunising, learning about diagnosing illness and prescribing medicines.

The break-up is a six week period in the spring when the ice breaks up and melts. In the little posts there are no airstrips so planes land on the ice in the winter and on water in the summer. They cannot land during the break-up, which means there is no contact with the outside world during those six weeks except by radio telephone, which apparently is not always reliable. Similarly, the freeze-up is a three month period in the autumn while the ice reforms. Fort Chimo is a big place with a runway so it is not affected by break-up and freeze-up.

Madame B has described Killinik to me: the Eskimos there are still living in very primitive conditions, some still in igloos and others in simple shacks. Most of them still live off the land hunting and fishing and travel around by dog teams or ski-doo (motorised sledge). Eskimos are apparently a very friendly and good-natured people and lovely to work with. She warned me that the first couple of weeks in the Arctic can be very difficult in such isolation and it is not uncommon for newcomers to pack up their belongings after a short time, ready to fly home. Being aware of this can help to adjust and accept the challenge. This has not dampened or diminished my enthusiasm in the least. I can hardly wait to get up there and especially to get into Killinik. I anticipate a thrilling year ahead of me!

March 1st 1969

I want to record now, before I leave, how I imagine the Arctic will be and later I can look back to compare my actual experience:

The Arctic; the unknown, that vast land of snow and ice and Eskimos. I'm going to live there for a year, a year of adventure and discovery. After reading *'DEW Line Doctor'* by Gareth Howerd, which has influenced me greatly, I have a vivid picture in my imagination of how it is going to be in Killinik: my little shack half under the snow, will have an open fire, a paraffin lamp, radio telephone and a few tins of food left by some previous dweller. The Eskimos will bring me their sick babies and I will visit the sick in their igloos, travelling by dog team. In my spare time, which will be in abundance, I shall read, write, paint and play my violin. I may even have time to do some teaching. I hope to learn the language to enable me to communicate in Eskimo. I plan to eat local produce and of course shall need Eskimo clothing. It will undoubtedly also be a year of self discovery. In just three days I shall be setting off on this adventure.

March 4th 1969

Today finally arrived! I have been given instructions to meet Kinalik at the airport and escort her to Fort Chimo. She is an Eskimo patient returning from Quebec to Wakeham Bay via Fort Chimo. I have also been given a list of messages for the doctor. All set to leave, I was notified at 9 a.m. that the flight had been cancelled so I have to wait another day. What a big disappointment, after all the build-up.

March 5th 1969
DORVAL AIRPORT MONTREAL

I arrived at the airport this morning complete with all my luggage for a year in the Arctic and collected Kinalik who was waiting for me as instructed at the Air Canada gateway. She speaks neither English nor French but we are communicating by smiles. I checked us in to the Nordair flight to Fort Chimo and was told that boarding the DC4 would be at 9.30. To my dismay, at 11 o'clock we were told that the flight would be cancelled until tomorrow morning, due to bad weather. Needless to say, I am bitterly disappointed. I phoned Madame B and she told me to take Kinalik to the Airport Inn where we should spend the night.

At the hotel I found 14 other people waiting for the flight to Fort Chimo, so it is a comfort not to be alone. Some of them have been here since yesterday and one family has been here more than a week. Flo and Doreen, two English Canadians, are here, each with two children, a couple of French Canadian men who are government employees, and Nancy, an Eskimo woman married to a white man is here with five of her eight children. At least Kinalik now has Nancy and her family to talk to. For myself, I am curious to find out more about Fort Chimo first-hand from Flo and Doreen, whose husbands have been based there working for the federal government for several years. From their description Fort Chimo sounds a very friendly informal sort of place. There are over 100 white people living and working there, from all walks of life.

Later we went down to the restaurant for a meal and I wondered what I could order for Kinalik. The chances of their having seal or whale meat were pretty remote so I thought fish might be the closest to Eskimo diet. I asked Nancy to ask Kinalik what she would like. Without the slightest hesitation she chose barbecued chicken and Coca-Cola. I was astounded.

This evening we have heard that the plane may be delayed again but we are optimistic that we will arrive by nightfall tomorrow. It is difficult to imagine they have such bad weather in Fort Chimo while we are basking in spring sunshine here.

March 6th 1969
DORVAL AIRPORT

We spent the morning hanging around the reception area anxiously waiting for news. All Nordair could tell us was that the storm was still raging. Finally they told us at 12.30 that we would be delayed for a further 24 hours. Another long day of waiting.

Apparently this sort of thing is not uncommon and in fact typifies the constant uncertainty of travelling in the north.

March 7th 1969
DORVAL AIRPORT

We killed time in the shopping centre yesterday afternoon and in the evening went to the International Hotel where there was a band and dancing. So we danced away our last night in civilisation. One of the men rang Nordair at 2 a.m. to find out what their news was. Not much change. So we carried on dancing.

We weren't surprised to learn today that the flight would be delayed for a further 24 hours. We are becoming resigned to staying indefinitely at the Airport Inn. Of course now that it is Friday it is possible Nordair won't fly in until Monday, even if the weather does clear.

March 8th 1969
FORT CHIMO

We celebrated another 'last evening in civilisation' at the International. Nordair's 2 a.m. report was still 'visibility almost zero with strong winds'. We went to bed despondently at 3.30.

We were woken at 7 a.m. to say that the plane was leaving at 9. Despite lack of sleep we were amazed and delighted to be given this news. The DC4 actually left on time. I have only flown three times before so the DC4 seemed very noisy after BOAC jets. It was impossible to have a conversation. It could also be like comparing being on a channel steamer with the Empress of Canada. We were 20 passengers in all, 16 of us destined for Fort Chimo and four for Frobisher Bay on Baffin Island. At midday we were served with a meal, not by an air hostess but by the co-pilot! Four hours after take-off, we started the descent to Fort Chimo; my heart was in my mouth. The big moment had finally arrived but suddenly it looked as if it were not to be: visibility had worsened and was now very poor. The plane rose again and headed north. Now, were we going to end up in Frobisher Bay? After a few minutes however, the plane turned back and finally landed without difficulty on Fort Chimo's airstrip.

March 15th 1969
FORT CHIMO

I have now been here a whole week. Little did I know that my first day was going to end in despair!

There were crowds of Eskimos in their fur-trimmed parkas, out to greet the plane. The first they had seen for a fortnight. The plane is apparently the big event of the week and everyone goes down to the airstrip. So this one, being so delayed, was very special. People are always curious to know who is on the plane, what provisions have come in and how many mail bags there are. It is their only link with civilisation.

As for myself, dressed in my entire skiing wardrobe, prepared for the freezing blast of breathtaking Arctic air, my first impression was rather a disappointment that it was much warmer than I had expected; between 20 and 30 degrees. I was also rather dismayed to see so many vehicles; jeeps, Land Rovers and ski-doos - not a dog team in sight. Dr l'Espérance and Georgette, one of the nurses, were there to meet me and my patient. Kinalik was sent to stay with an Eskimo family while waiting to go back to her own village. I was going to miss my silent, smiling companion. I was taken in one of the Land Rovers to the 'Centre', where provincial government employees live. It is about four miles to the village from the airstrip and we bumped along the snow-covered track for about 20 minutes. I was deposited at the Centre, shown to my room and left to my own devices.

My room seemed bare and unwelcoming: a bed, wooden chair, coffee table and a wash basin. No curtains or floor covering. I felt abandoned and desolate wondering what I had let myself in for. As my luggage had not yet arrived I had nothing to do so I lay on the bed with the door open, hoping someone would come and talk to me and I tried to think about what it was going to be like once I was settled in Killinik. After all, Fort Chimo was only temporary. Somewhere down the corridor a girl was trying to give her dog a bath in a sink. She was having a conversation and laughing with someone else while the dog struggled to get out of the water. Their conversation seemed inane to me and I felt excluded. Another snappy little dog was wandering up and down restlessly and passed my door several times without so much as a glance in my direction. Suddenly it vomited on the floor. I got up and closed my door. "What a place!" I thought, "What am I doing here?" This wasn't how I had imagined the Arctic. I felt thoroughly disconsolate.

At 4 p.m. Paulette, the nurse in charge, came to introduce herself and apologise for not having been able to meet me at the plane. She could now spend some time with me so I immediately felt better. It was a relief to talk to her and I had a lot of questions to ask. When I had previously mentioned to others that I was only spending six weeks here before going to Killinik for the year, there had been uncomfortable silence and exchanged looks. Paulette seemed embarrassed so I asked her what was going on. She told me frankly, that like many others, I had been misled. Most people spend the year in Fort Chimo and might be lucky to be sent to a small post for four weeks. I told her I had specifically requested a small post and had been promised Killinik for the break-up. The final blow was when Paulette told me that Killinik doesn't even come under our jurisdiction so that is definitely out of the question. I was stunned and angry. I had been sent up here under false pretences. The fact that I was not the first was no consolation.

Paulette showed me around the Centre and the little hospital which takes up a whole wing of the Centre. That evening all the residents gathered together in the sitting room for a party. I learned later that it was mainly in my honour but no-one was feeling in a party mood. I felt uncomfortable because I could feel the strained atmosphere. There was a kind of depressed resignation and apathy. The apathy frightened me more than anything. Was this how the Arctic affected you? Would I end up like this after a year, if I stayed? Nobody seemed to have any vitality. My misgivings were increasing by the hour. I was surely making a big mistake. So ended my first day in the Arctic. The day I had yearned for so long. My dream had been shattered and my reason for being in Fort Chimo had already disintegrated. Killinik was not to be mine after all. I was a victim of gross deception.

Despite the events of my first day, I slept well, possibly as a result of all our 'last evenings in civilisation'. As I awoke, the memories of the day before filtered through my consciousness and I wondered what my second day would bring. At least I would be occupied working with Paulette in the hospital that morning.

In the afternoon I went on some home visits with Louise, another nurse and Mary, one of the Eskimo interpreters. Louise took the names, addresses and symptoms of the patients we were to visit, collected her black bag and we set off in the little hospital Jeep. It is apparently usually impossible to drive right up to houses so we drove as far as possible and walked the rest of the way through the snow. Louise examined the patients, asking questions through the interpreter, then phoned Dr l'Espérance who prescribed treatment over the phone. Louise had a good supply of medicines ready in the bag. She has been here over 10 months now and is very competent. I am rather nervous about going out on my own but I have been assured that I can accompany the experienced nurses until I feel confident. Dr l'Espérance is very nice and encourages us to take responsibility. It seems strange to be working through an interpreter, it is quite time-consuming but I expect I shall get used to it. The other interpreter is Louisa. Their help is invaluable as we have to be able to identify the patients' problems as accurately as possible. Patients phone the hospital when they are ill and the nurse visiting will collect as much information as possible before going out.

The first thing that struck me was the very strong smell which permeated the houses, from raw seal meat and skins which are stored in the entrance porches. Most Eskimos live in primitive shacks but the government is beginning to supply prefabricated houses which arrive by ship in the summer. Apparently no-one actually lives in igloos any more but if they go out hunting and are away for a night they have to build a temporary igloo, otherwise they would die of exposure. They have very little furniture in their houses, mainly a bed or two (several people sleep on each bed) and boxes. People sit around on beds or boxes. Clothes seem to be piled in boxes or hung across the room on string. The shacks now all have oil-fired stoves (the government supplies the oil) so it feels very warm inside them. In many houses small children are running around in their underwear. Apparently children soon learn the danger of frostbite outside and leaving them in their underwear is a way of keeping them inside.

There aren't many Huskies around now and those that are have to be chained up unless they are working, as they can be dangerous. Sometimes at night they all start howling together in harmony which is quite eerie as they sound like wolves.

Fort Chimo Eskimos are apparently very dependant on the government and although a few still go out hunting and fishing, most don't have anything to do unless they are involved in handicrafts or selling skins. Some of course, do work for the government, for example interpreters and cleaners. Most are given welfare money every week.

The village spreads over about a square mile and is just below the tree line so trees here are thin and puny. Further north of course are no trees at all. Apart from the road to the airstrip which is always kept open, there are no other roads. The best, almost permanent tracks made by ski-doos, lead to the Hudson's Bay Company store (now called 'the Bay') and the Anglican church. The Bay seems to be the focal point of the village; it is always full of people and a popular meeting place. It sells everything from sewing thread to ski-doos, including canned foods, clothing, skins, household goods, fishing tackle, guns and canoes. We can have an account there so there is no need to carry cash.

Most institutions seem to be duplicated; the Eskimo co-op store which is run by Eskimos with guidance from the headquarters in Quebec City, sells handicrafts, skins and furs and other clothing. A good deal of produce, especially handicrafts such as prints, soap stone, whale bone and ivory carvings,

Eskimo parkas and seal skin wares are exported down south and are an important source of income.

Of the two churches, the Anglican church is attended by the majority of the Eskimo population. There are several services on Sundays and some during the week. The Roman Catholic mission has been here for over 20 years but most of the Eskimos here are Anglican. It seems that when missionaries started coming to the Arctic, it was a question of whichever arrived first, converted first.

Pou-pou, so named by the Eskimos, is a Belgian missionary and has been here for 20 years. When he first arrived he was appalled to see heads crawling with lice and exclaimed with horror "Des poux! Des poux!" No-one seems to know what his real name is; Pou-pou has stuck. He is quite a character.

There are two police stations: the RCMP (Royal Canadian Mounted Police - needless to say, un-mounted here) and the provincial police. There are also two schools, federal and provincial. Both are modern and well equipped. José, one of the teachers, took me on a tour of the provincial school. I was interested to see some of the drawings and paintings done by Eskimo children. The detail, movement and expression they include are incredible. I was particularly impressed with a drawing by one of José's seven-year-old pupils. It was simply a picture of a mother with a baby in the 'amauti' hood. (The amauti is a special parka with a large hood which holds the baby on the mother's back).

Somehow this child had managed to capture the motherly look on the mother's face and a contented look on the baby's. Eskimo children are very observant and are soon able to mimic different mannerisms they observe in we whites (kadluna). They are friendly and come running up to us and ask, "Kina uvit?" ("Who are you?") The Eskimos call me Annie, so I can say, "Annie uvunga".

The Centre houses all the provincial government employees: nurses, electricians, the cook, lab. technician, radio telephone operator, plumbers, mechanics, engineers and construction workers. The teachers have their meals here but sleep in their own accommodation. Our rooms are all at one end of the Centre, along the same corridor. There are no closed doors, it is really communal living! We each have our own washbasins but share the shower, bath and toilets. The shower is out of order most of the time and the bathroom is situated between Bob's room and the cook's and the only access is through one of those rooms. Bob is the radio telephone operator, he is very easy-going and also sleeps very deeply so he doesn't mind and is probably completely unaware of the traffic through his room. As there are no locks on the bathroom doors, someone has come up with the idea of a plank of wood which you simply lay across the bathroom floor to block both doors. We also have a sitting room. All this accommodation is centrally heated.

There is a large dining room and the first thing that struck me was the tins of Carnation milk on each table. Of course there is no fresh milk here. I am already getting used to Carnation on my cereal and in drinks. The food is quite good. There is plenty of fresh frozen meat, tinned fruit and vegetables and the cook bakes fresh bread, cakes and biscuits every day. He is quite a character and manages to feed us all with only three Eskimo girls to help him with the washing up. If he is in a good mood he sings the same unmelodious tune all day long. When he is under the influence of alcohol (which I gather is not uncommon) he apparently sits in the dining room swearing and shouting at everyone in sight. In these instances, we have to fend for ourselves and cook whatever we can find until he resumes his role as cook a few days later. After the evening meal we often have Eskimo children visiting and selling crafts, especially seal skin 'Ookpiks' (Arctic Owls). I find the ookpiks irresistible and have already bought three.

As well as our accommodation and the hospital, there is a lab., an X-ray room, stock room and a laundry room where we can use the washing machines and drying machines. Soap and washing powder are even provided free of charge.

The hospital is only two years old and is very well equipped: four patient rooms; one with three adult beds, the others with children's cots and an incubator; a small kitchen, bathroom and office. Downstairs is the outpatient clinic. Eileen is an English nurse and midwife and she runs the outpatient clinic. She is married to Bernard who is French Canadian and works for the DOT (Department of Transport). They have only recently moved here and are expecting their first baby soon. A very nice couple. We (the other nurses) work three shifts, one on each shift, and have two days off a week if there are enough of us. If not, the one who has a day off has to do the home visits, as is the case at the moment. We may occasionally get the opportunity to fly out to one of the smaller outposts if there is a medical emergency. Yesterday we heard about a man who was badly burned and one of us was to fly out to fetch him. Unfortunately our weather was bad but the pilot was able to fly him to the hospital in Frobisher Bay. We also have to take radio telephone messages that come in from nurses in the outposts. The radio telephone is just through the swing doors of the hospital corridor so we work to a constant background of crackling, unintelligible voices. At first, it seemed to me that Bob was having endless conversations with or about someone called Roger. I have since learned that 'roger' is the code for 'understood', 'message received' or 'OK' Inevitably, all radio conversations are peppered with 'rogers'. 'Negative copy' means 'not understood', 'over and out' is the end of the conversation. Whenever I have been on duty and messages have come in from nurses in other outposts, Bob has had to take messages for me as I can't yet pick anything intelligible out of the crackles but he is very patient and used to all the medical language by now.

I shall have to get some Eskimo clothing made. The atigi (a knee-length parka) is made of two layers; the outer windproof is called the silapak and decorated with braid round the hem and cuffs. The inner is made of duffel with fur (usually fox) round the hood and sometimes round the cuffs. A brooch, made of beadwork may be used to pin the two hoods together. In summer either of these garments may be worn separately. The amauti is worn by a woman carrying a baby. The extra large hood, surrounded by fur, accommodates the baby. The baby can be swivelled round to the breast without being exposed to the outside air. Kamiks are sealskin boots which have duffel liners. A horizontal pattern is incorporated into kamiks for females and a vertical design for males, whether adults or babies. Sometimes it is the only way you can tell the sex of someone all dressed up outside! Kamiks are snow-proof but not waterproof. In the summer rubber boots are worn.

March 19th 1969

I have now been here eleven days and despite my original despair, time has gone by quickly as we are very busy and it is so different from the south. I am really enjoying the experience. On Monday the new Nordair Jet came, the first time there has ever been a jet here. Everyone was at the airstrip, there was an air of excitement and the weather was fine. The jet had no trouble landing but the fire engine was out, just in case. From now on we should get two planes a week. The jet takes only two hours from Montreal.

I have been to the Bay to buy the materials for my atigi: navy blue gabardine, duffel, braids, embroidery threads and a whole fox fur which cost $7.50. I took all these materials round to Eva Adams who is going to make my atigi. She is apparently one of the best Eskimo needlewomen here. She measured me with lengths of wool which she broke off with her teeth before laying each length neatly on the table afterwards. She will remember which is which! I asked her to embroider the duffel however she liked so it will be a spontaneous work of art.

On Sunday evening I decided to go to the Anglican church. It was a freezing cold evening, about 30 below with high winds, which with the chill factor was the equivalent of about 60 below. Even with my sheepskin coat and fur hat the wind penetrated. I shall be glad when I have my atigi. After a ten minute walk, I was thankful to be inside the church. It is very simple inside, with wooden benches, an altar and a stove. I was the first to arrive so sat near the stove. After a few minutes a couple of Eskimos arrived and disappeared upstairs. Then other Eskimos came crowding in with their children. Eventually, the two ministers came downstairs in their robes and the service (in Eskimo) began. It went on for almost two hours. There were Bible readings and hymns which were vaguely recognisable but sung in a slow monotonous kind of drone. Children were running around all over the place and jumping over the benches. Many of the adults were coughing and some had brought old tins which they placed at their feet and periodically spat into them with perfect aim. At the end of the service, after the final blessing which was interspersed with coughing, screaming babies and bottles crashing to the floor, the two ministers went upstairs but no-one made a move to go. About ten minutes later the ministers, now in their outdoor clothing, came downstairs and shook hands with everyone as they filed out in a very orderly fashion, row by row starting with the front row. It was only later that I realised that men sat on the left and women and children on the right. I had sat by the stove which was on the left.

I am getting to know my way around now and feel confident doing home visits. We get plenty of calls for home visits. Most of the calls are for sick children. Bronchitis, otitis, diarrhoea and vomiting are the commonest problems. Some houses are quite clean and others very dirty by our standards. I went to one house the other day where a young man was sitting on one of the beds mending a ski-doo motor!

On Friday Louisette (a nurse) and I went out for a ride in the little hospital jeep. We spotted a group of children sliding off a roof in the snow. "What a wonderful photo that would be," I said. By the time we stopped the jeep and appeared with our cameras the children were all standing in a straight line smiling. Not quite the spontaneous photo I had anticipated but they were cute.

We continued down to Lake Stewart where the road ends and there we found Bernard (Eileen's husband) and Pou-pou with their ski-doos. They were just about to have a little 20 minute trip across the lake and back again so invited us to go with them. It was such a lovely afternoon we accepted with pleasure. We sat on Bernard's trailer behind his ski-doo and followed Pou-pou on his. It was a very bumpy ride. After about half an hour we realised to our horror that we were lost! We had gone through some woods at the end of the lake and thinking we had turned round at that point, were surprised not to see our tracks. We had all had faith in Pou-pou who was leading the way, as he has been here so many years. We spent quite a time searching for our tracks and by now the sun had set so we had no landmarks to guide us, just a vast expanse of white. I must confess I was quite frightened, my feet had already frozen and were numb. Neither Louisette nor I had our ski-doo suits on as it was only going to be a short trip across the lake, to the woods and back again. I started to wonder if we would have to spend the night out there and how long we could survive. It seemed pretty hopeless. All of a sudden we found some tracks, by now just visible, and followed them. To our great relief they were ours. I could have wept for joy to see our little jeep waiting for us. We realised later, looking at the map, that we had come out on another lake parallel to Lake Stewart after the woods and we were heading for the Ungava Bay! Neither Louisette nor I were capable of driving as we both had frozen legs up to our thighs. At least we had warm jackets. Bernard drove us back to the Centre in our jeep.

It was tempting to get into a hot bath to thaw out but we knew that would be dangerous. It was when the feeling began to return to our limbs that the pain began. We were dancing around in agony for about 20 minutes, it was impossible to stay still. Although we weren't seriously frozen, it has made me realise how dangerous it could have been and always to wear a ski-doo suit in future, even on short trips. I have learned my lesson.

Freezing to death is apparently the most comfortable way to die. Once the feeling has gone, one starts to become sleepy and gradually coma takes over. In the old days, when Eskimos were travelling around with dog teams, living a more nomadic lifestyle, it was important that everyone could contribute so that when the old people became a burden to the family, they would often volunteer to be left behind in the igloo and would freeze to death. Of course, in our situation, it would have been imperative to stay awake if we had had to spend the night out.

Pou-pou has a little chalet down by the lake and offered it to any of us who are off for the weekend so José, Lucie, Alain (all teachers) and I went down on Saturday afternoon to spend the night there. Pou-pou drove us down on the road as far as he could and we walked the rest of the way on snow shoes. Another new experience for me! The chalet is just a little hut with a couple of beds, a table, chair and cooker. No electricity or water of course. We had to melt snow to make water. Pou-pou lit the stove, assured us there was plenty of oil for the night and left us to it. Jacquie (a new nurse), joined us later, bringing with her a bottle of Vodka. We had the Arctic sleeping bags, three among five of us so Jacquie had one and the rest of us spread out one under us and one over us and snuggled up together. At some stage during the night the stove went out. Alain and I who were at the outside ends of the sleeping bag, were the first to notice that it was very cold and we suspected the stove had gone out but neither of us had the courage to investigate. We just snuggled closer together towards the others in the middle of the sleeping bag. It took a lot of courage to emerge from our cosy nest the next morning but we were greeted by the most spectacular sight of an inch of frost on all the trees. It was so beautiful! Apparently this only happens when there is a dramatic drop in temperature and I think it did drop to about 50 below that night. We walked on the lake for an hour to warm ourselves up a bit and then went back to the chalet to cook eggs and bacon. After innumerable trips fetching snow we finally managed to heat enough water to do the washing up. We donned our snow shoes and walked back to the road where Pou-pou had arranged to pick us up and take us back to the Centre. Despite the chill, it was refreshing to 'get away from it all' for a night.

March 26th 1969

I have been working on night duty the last couple of weeks. Usually there isn't much to do unless the babies wake up. We do all the sterilising and stock-taking at night. Last night a woman arrived in labour and the delivery went well. The doctor has to be called when a woman is in Stage Two labour or if there are any problems in Stage One and he does the delivery. Canadian nurses don't do midwifery.

When all is quiet, we can go down to the dining room and make ourselves something to eat. The cook always leaves plenty of fresh dripping out. One night about 3 am I went down to make myself some toast and dripping and I found the cook, very drunk, trying to let himself into the kitchen, fumbling with his keys which he subsequently dropped on the floor. He seemed to think it was breakfast time and I had a job to persuade him it wasn't. Eventually, as he was so confused, I took him to his room and put him to bed. I knew that we would be doing our own cooking for a few days!

The sun rises about 5 a.m. and the frost on the office window (inside and out) makes fantastic patterns with the sun shining through.

We had a drama one evening; three of us were having a chat when suddenly an Eskimo lad accompanied by two white lads, arrived at the hospital. Joe, one of the white lads was very shaken and trembling. He had been riding with his friend Jan (who is married to Lydia, an Eskimo woman) on a ski-doo, when he (Joe) fell off. The Eskimo lad was so close behind on his ski-doo that he ran over Joe who apart from being shaken had no other injuries. Joe was given a tranquilliser and sent home. A few minutes later we heard a woman moaning and groaning, coming upstairs. It sounded as if she was in labour. It was Lydia, Jan's wife, with a friend, both very drunk, having heard about the accident and fearing the worst. We managed to reassure them that they were fine and everyone went home. The day after the plane has come is often pretty eventful as alcohol arrives and fights may ensue. The police are always busy on these days. The evening shift is usually the busiest as the outpatient department is closed so people just turn up at the hospital.

April 2nd 1969

We have had a busy week this week. We had a super party on Saturday at the Duponts'. He is the DOT cook. There was a marvellous punch and a good selection of records. We danced 'till about 4 a.m. On Sunday I helped Louise pack her trunk as she is going to Wakeham Bay for the break-up.

On Friday, Mary, Eva Adams' daughter, came to tell me that my atigi was finished so I went round later to Eva's house to collect it and pay her. It is a perfect fit and the embroidery is absolutely gorgeous. She has embroidered fantasy flowers all over the duffel. As Mary wasn't there to interpret, all I could do was say, "Nakomik", (Thankyou) "Piojoq! Piojoq!" (Beautiful!). Eva seemed very pleased. I am thrilled.

I bought some corduroy jeans at the Bay last week. It's amazing how much pleasure can be derived from small things like that. I was as excited as if I had bought an evening dress. Little pleasures become big events here.

On Monday I was told that there were three patients going south on the plane and it was my turn to go out on escort. At first I didn't want to go; I was just getting settled and didn't want to see civilisation again yet. However, I had to go. The plane left at 7.30 p.m. I had a dehydrated three-week-old baby and two pregnant women to take to Quebec. The two women, Mary and Annie, came from other settlements but the baby had been in our hospital on intravenous fluids which were disconnected just before the flight. We had to go up to Frobisher Bay first, just an hour's flight from Fort Chimo. It is much bigger than Chimo, they even have taxis! Their airstrip is lit by electric lights whereas ours is lit by paraffin flares. This already felt like civilisation to me. We left there at 9.30 p.m. and got to Montreal at 12.30 a.m. I still had to get to Quebec and there were two men, government employees, also destined for Quebec. A government taxi was waiting for us, so we knew that would take another two hours on the autoroute. The driver set off at a snail's pace and didn't seem to know the way although once on the autoroute it was clearly straight on all the way. At every slip road, he slowed down and hesitated. One of the men in front kept telling him it was straight on but it didn't seem to make much difference. After about an hour, the taxi skidded into the side of the road. We had a puncture! All the luggage had to come out of the back and the three men set to to change the wheel. I stayed in my seat with the baby who was sleeping peacefully. We eventually set off again but had to stop to get the wheel repaired as soon as we saw a garage. We had some coffee while waiting for the repair. There were still

130 miles to go and fortunately one of the men managed to persuade the driver to let him drive, which he did, quite willingly. We reached the outskirts of Quebec about 5 a.m. and I was dropped off at the Hôpital St Sacrement where Mary and the baby were admitted after I had filled out masses of forms, which I was not too happy about at 5.30 in the morning. Annie and I were to stay in a nearby house which had been previously arranged, for what was left of the 'night'.

After a few hours' sleep I rang Madame B to ask when I was to go to Montreal. She had booked me on the 1.15 p.m. flight and I was thankful not to have to spend four hours on the train. She brought my ticket round to me. I tried to get her to tell me when I would be going to my little outpost and she was rather evasive about the break-up but promised me somewhere for the freeze-up. Anyway, now I have got used to Chimo so it doesn't seem so bad. The summer promises to be very busy with all the immunisations and X-rays. The flight only took 35 minutes to Montreal so that was wonderful.

I bought a new camera in Montreal, a Minolta S.R.T.101, one of the best on the market apparently. Unfortunately I couldn't take it with me as they have to wait until the cheque is cleared but they will send it to me. Tonight I have to go to the airport, collect two patients and spend the night (or ? several nights…) at the Airport Inn ready to fly back tomorrow morning.

Author with Fort Chimo hospital jeep

April 10th 1969
FORT CHIMO

After my short trip to Montreal there have been quite a few changes here. Louise has gone to Wakeham Bay for the break-up and Louisette suddenly had to go home as her sister is terminally ill. She won't be coming back apparently. I shall miss them both as we all got on so well together. Louisette played the piano and sometimes we would go to the school and play violin and piano duets. Occasionally Louise came along too and listened and we once gave her a recital over the phone when she was on evening duty with no patients. Lorraine (whom I haven't met yet), is in George River but may only stay there a month so there is a possibility that I may go there for the break-up. (Dare I hope?) The cook has gone south for a week's holiday and we have no replacement so we will be doing our own cooking again for awhile.

I had a cold bath this morning as there is no hot water. At least our water in the Centre is not rationed; some houses have small tanks and despite the daily water delivery, it is not always enough. Most of the Eskimos have plastic barrels with a tap which contain about 45 gallons, others fetch water as they need it. We are lucky. With permafrost it is impossible to have underground pipes, so every house has a water tank for clean water.

I have been trying to learn some Eskimo (Inuktituk) but it is much more difficult than any of the European languages I know. There was no written language when the first missionaries came to the Arctic so someone devised a syllabic language based on Pitman's shorthand. The English and French written versions vary quite a bit so that is another problem. Inuktituk is spoken right across the Arctic from Alaska to Greenland, with some different dialects but the same basic language. For example here, 'white man' is 'kadluna', in other places it could be 'kabluna' or 'kapluna'.

Over Easter we managed to empty the hospital and we have taken it in turns to be on call. We can plug the hospital phone into our rooms as we all have phone sockets in our rooms. On

Easter Monday some of us went to spend the afternoon with Pou-pou in his chalet and we cooked a meal there. It was a glorious afternoon.

April 16th 1969

Mary, our interpreter, has been helping me with Eskimo and I now know about 50 words or phrases although I don't yet understand much when it is spoken. They seem to understand me though.

I have delivered my first Eskimo baby! Louise 2, one of the new nurses, was on night duty when Harriet turned up in labour. Louise has had no midwifery experience so she came to wake me at 4 a.m. to ask me to examine the patient. There was no time to get the doctor as Harriet was in advanced labour and I delivered her within a few minutes, still in my nightdress with a white coat over it. A lovely delivery and a beautiful little girl, Elizabeth Kudlu. I was too excited to sleep the rest of the night, having brought my first beautiful little Eskimo baby into the world.

The cook is still away but Maurice the electrician has been doing the cooking. Unfortunately he managed to slice a bit off the end of a finger in the bread slicing machine yesterday so I had to bandage him up and take him off kitchen duties, much to his disappointment as he was enjoying himself. In the meantime M. Dupont, the DOT cook is going to help out.

The weather has been gorgeous this week and tomorrow I'm hoping to go over to Old Chimo with Flo. We want to see the musk ox farm. I haven't seen much of Flo since we first met at Dorval Airport. The river ice is about two feet thick at the moment.

I may be going to George River about 5th May - weather permitting of course.

April 20th 1969

I have now had my first experience of suturing. Last night about 1.45 a.m. a 19-year-old Eskimo man had a ski-doo accident and gashed his leg. He was very patient as I had to make do with very fine thread (normally used for plastic surgery) as we had run out of the usual. As a result, the thread kept breaking and the first needle broke too. I think it will heal well as it was a clean tear.

On Thursday Flo and I went over to Old Chimo on our ski-doos. Sandy, an Eskimo who lives over there came here to take us over. An exciting 45 minute trip. It was snowing so it was good that Sandy could lead the way as we might have lost the track across the river, had we been on our own. The worst bits are at the edges of the river where the ice is like frozen boulders. Once in the middle of the river it is quite smooth. I must confess to feeling very nervous seeing some of the deep crevasses and hearing the ice cracking from time to time. I breathed a sigh of relief on reaching land.

Old Chimo, which is seven miles down river from Fort Chimo, has an interesting history: originally, it was a Hudson's Bay trading post. Eskimos and Cree Indians were living over there together. The government decided to separate them so the Eskimos were resettled in Fort Chimo and the Cree moved further south to a place called Schefferville. Apparently the Indians were all suffering from chest conditions and I suppose the climate further south would be more therapeutic. Now, there is only one Eskimo family left in Old Chimo and they help with the musk ox farm.

Diederik and Joan are in charge of the farm and they came to meet us and welcomed us with a cup of coffee. They showed us around the farm where they have 14 head: three bulls and eleven females, all three years old. In 1967 there was an expedition to Ellesmere Island with the goal of catching twelve female and three male calves. This took two weeks but the goal was achieved. (One must have died later). They are hoping to start breeding this year. The musk oxen have beautiful long thick coats with a silky undercoat called qiviut. Joan is teaching Eskimo women to knit and weave qiviut. The Eskimos have always known that qiviut is even warmer than goose down. The musk oxen are about the size of Shetland ponies, now quite tame and will let you touch them. The only other farm is in Alaska where they have 24 head. There are apparently some 10,000 running wild in the Arctic but they are extremely nervous and a helicopter frightens them so much that they panic and scatter in all directions, so are very difficult (and expensive) to catch.

While we were there we suddenly spotted a woman and child who appeared in difficulty on the river. Diederik took his ski-doo and went out to them. They had had to abandon their ski-doo among the 'boulders' so he brought them back with him. On our return to Fort Chimo we met the woman's husband who had found the ski-doo and was on his way to fetch them both. Sandy reassured him they were OK.

I have heard the most fascinating story about Fort Chimo: in 1939 apparently a secret hospital was built there, with 300 rooms. It must have been enormous! It was built by the Canadian and American Air Force who flew around picking up wounded soldiers and other war casualties from many different countries, bringing them to this ultramodern hospital. The only criteria were that patients must know their names and addresses. The location of the hospital was kept secret from patients and possibly from some of the staff. The patients were flown home again after treatment. The hospital was guarded day and night by the RCMP. Of course there were no Eskimos living there at that time as they were still in Old Chimo. In 1946 the hospital, all equipment and vehicles were completely destroyed. Traces of vehicles have been found under rocks where they were hidden. What an amazing story! I wonder how many patients and nurses have been to the Canadian Arctic without knowing it. What a waste though, to have destroyed everything. I don't understand why they had to do that.

April 22nd 1969

The cook still has not returned after his 'week's' holiday! (12 days ago now).

Our feature film this week was *'The King and I'*. I had always regretted not seeing it in 1956, like everyone else, so there are advantages of having old films. It was very good.

I have just heard that I am definitely going to George River for the break-up, probably on Thursday (only a few days away!). The break-up should start in May, so I will be there until July. Once the break-up starts the pilots take six weeks' holiday, so I shall really be totally out of contact with the outside world for at least six weeks. I'm longing to experience that!

April 26th 1969

I was supposed to have gone into George River on Thursday but there was no plane. It will probably be next week now.

Spring is really in the air this week. Temperatures are now in the 30s in the daytime but still drop to about zero at night. Snow is beginning to melt which means we will soon have to start wearing rubber boots as kamiks are not waterproof. There is no Bay store in George River so I shall have to stock up before I go. The nurse there has to live with the provincial administrator's family (a couple with an eight-year-old daughter) so I won't have to buy food.

In the early hours of Thursday morning I delivered another baby. Eileen, who is a midwife, was also on night duty, so there were two of us. The patient had a post partum haemorrhage the next day and we had to round up some volunteers to give blood. Fortunately the lab. has facilities for this. Luckily the mother recovered and is now fine.

The doctor went south on Thursday so I am working in the outpatient department which is very interesting. We have a good supply of medical text books, such as differential diagnosis, treatments and prescribing drugs etc. and I have my own midwifery text book. Eileen is still around to help with any deliveries too. Yesterday a woman arrived in labour and we didn't know she was pregnant. She delivered a premature baby, 3 lbs 10 oz but both mother and baby are fine.

Fort Chimo: children lined up for photo

April 27th 1969

We have just had a very dramatic 24 hours! Yesterday afternoon Louise called from Wakeham Bay to say she had a woman with retained placenta after delivery. She could not leave her patient so Paulette and Eileen were sending messages and instructions over the radio telephone to the administrator in Wakeham Bay who then had to get these messages to Louise while she also reported back. Long-winded communication. The patient was bleeding and in shock. Two hours later Paulette managed to get a little Beechcraft plane to go in and fetch them here. It is a two hour trip to Wakeham Bay. Eileen and I went to meet the plane later with the ambulance, not knowing what to expect, as we had not been able to have any radio contact since. We had organised some blood donors in the meantime. When the plane arrived the patient (Alacie) was in poor condition and Louise was exhausted. We drove as quickly as possible back to the hospital and set up a blood transfusion in one arm and intravenous fluids in the other before getting Alacie ready to fly to Schefferville. The pilot was happy to continue flying the Beech to Schefferville, 300 miles further south, where there is a hospital with several doctors and operating facilities.

I escorted Alacie in the plane and took Jacquie, one of the new nurses, with me to help. Alacie was on a stretcher on the floor. Jacquie and I sat on the floor, one on each side of her. There wasn't much room to move around in the little Beech. We left about 7 p.m. From time to time we had to administer oxygen when it looked as if we might lose Alacie. However, we arrived in time and an ambulance was there to meet us to take us to the hospital which was only five minutes away. We were welcomed with a café cognac! We were then shown around the hospital which is very modern: 35 beds, a delivery room and operating theatre.

Schefferville (which is where the Old Chimo Indians now live), was built as a mining town fairly recently. The area is rich in iron. They have no roads to the south but they have a railway with three trains a week as well as a daily plane in the winter and two planes a day in the summer. Not as isolated as Chimo but they consider themselves isolated. By the time we left at 10.30 p.m. Alacie was doing well. At 1 a.m. we were back in Chimo.

May 6th 1969

I am STILL in Fort Chimo! We have had such a hectic ten days that I really didn't feel I could leave Paulette on her own, with newly qualified nurses, now that Eileen has left to have her baby and the doctor hasn't come back yet. I am the only one with midwifery experience so I volunteered to look after the outpatient clinic and midwifery cases. Paulette was very grateful; she and I work very well together.

I have delivered three more babies this week and the clinic has been very busy too. I am loving it despite the fact that I'm longing to get to George River. On Saturday Paulette was to take a baby with convulsions to Schefferville so I drove her to the plane. When the pilot told her that they might not be returning to Chimo straightaway, Paulette just handed me the baby and said I would have to go! She couldn't leave for more than a day. It was only a week since I had been to Schefferville, in the same Beechcraft. The baby didn't have any more convulsions and I handed him over to the hospital. Alacie was ready to come home and it was wonderful to see her so well after having been at death's door only a week ago. I was invited round to one of the doctor's houses where he and his wife entertained me while I waited for the plane. The plane left at 5.30 p.m., circled round in freezing fog for half an hour and landed again at Schefferville. Alacie was taken back to the ward and I was taken to the nurses' home. We had a wonderful meal with trout and there was real milk to drink too. I rarely drink milk normally but after so long with Carnation I found the real thing delicious. I borrowed soap and a towel from the hospital and one of the nurses lent me some pyjamas. (After all, I had only set out to take Paulette to the plane, so only had the clothes I stood up in). Everyone was so friendly. The next morning was very stormy so we didn't leave until 3 p.m. We arrived safely in Chimo two hours later. I now don't know when I'm going to get to George River as Paulette is going south on escort but the doctor is due back any time. It has been very hot this week and the snow is melting fast. I hope there will be another plane to George River before it is too late. I am still waiting for my new camera to arrive too.

The jet has not been the success we anticipated! Now the snow has melted and left the airstrip in such bad condition it is apparently damaging the jet as gravel flies up into the works. So, no more jets.

May 9th 1969

I have just heard that the last plane is going into George River at 6 a.m. tomorrow.

George River: mail plane

CHAPTER 2
GEORGE RIVER

May 11th 1969

At last I have made it here! Having been on tenterhooks for three weeks I was beginning to wonder if I would ever see George River. I was supposed to be leaving at 6 a.m. yesterday and was not surprised to find myself still in Chimo at 9.00. Anything was possible. At 10.30 they came to tell me they were leaving in half an hour. Paulette took me down to the plane and it finally took off at 11.30.

The little twin engine Beechcraft was packed right up to the roof with mail, food and other last minute provisions for the break-up. It was to be the last plane for several weeks. All the passenger seats had been removed and every inch of space was filled. I had to climb up on the wing and through the cockpit to take my seat beside Johnny May, an Eskimo pilot. We finally set off for this 80 mile trip across the Ungava Bay. The clouds were low so we flew at about 700 feet all the way which gave us a fantastic view of the landscape, rivers and lakes. We followed the coast most of the way and as we turned inland towards George River the wind was pretty strong and I secretly wondered if we would make it. Johnny pointed out the village to me as we descended. There were only a few patches of snow left in the village and the handful of houses were barely visible against the dull brown background. We circled twice round the village and I held my breath. Would this be another weekend in Fort Chimo? Johnny is an excellent pilot though, quite fearless and a bit of a dare devil, I gather. Under quite difficult conditions, with wind and the state of the ice, he made a perfect landing on skis on the river. The surface of the ice was melting fast and was covered with water which sprayed around us as we landed. When the plane was at a standstill Johnny opened the cockpit, climbed out on to his wing and jumped down. I climbed out my side and was terrified at the thought of jumping into that water. It looked very deep from that height. Johnny laughed and came to help me down. I was relieved to find that it wasn't that deep, it didn't even feel slippery. Looking towards the village, we saw a swarm of little black dots that after a few minutes materialised into ski-doos, coming to meet the plane. Very quickly everything was skillfully loaded and firmly tied on to the komautiks (a sledge-like trailer pulled by ski-doo). Claude, the administrator, whose family I am living with for the next few weeks, came out to meet me. Lorraine, the nurse who I am replacing, just had time to wish me luck before taking her place beside Johnny for the trip back to Chimo.

My luggage had been distributed among various komautiks and in view of the wet conditions I decided to hold on to the violin myself. Johnny Annanak, apparently one of the best drivers, took me on his ski-doo. There were quite a few patches of deep water to negotiate and the ice seemed to be visibly melting under the afternoon sun. It took about 40 minutes to reach the village. All the Eskimos were there to greet me and there was a lot of "Anniengai" ("Hello Annie") and handshaking. What a lovely welcome. Johnny took me to Claude's house and his wife France was there to welcome me. I am sharing eight-year-old Véronique's bedroom as they only have two bedrooms. She is a chatty little girl and I'm sure we will get on fine. The family seems very relaxed and they told me just to make myself at home.

I am glad to have taken my violin with me because one of my suitcases arrived waterlogged and I had to dry everything out. Luckily it was mainly clothing.

There are only seven white people here and as I have briefly met Carolyne, a teacher, I only have a couple more to meet. The Eskimo population is about 220. I have already had six patients despite the fact that it is Saturday, but as no-one had anything serious I think it was a case of seeing what the new nurse was like! I am already feeling at home here.

Carolyne with her class

May 12th 1969

It's a strange feeling knowing you are cut off from civilisation for two months. It is rather like being on a desert island I should imagine. Apart from the radio telephone which is unreliable anyway, we have no radio, television or telephone here. The radio telephone is on all day and actually sounds clearer here than at Chimo. There is less interference. Electricity is powered by a generator in the village and water is delivered weekly.

I realised when I unpacked my clothes that I had left my pants behind so I radioed Paulette just in case there is another plane. It was a very bad connection and I had to repeat myself several times so by now, the whole coast must know that the nurse is 'pantiless'. I shall just have to make do with the two pairs I have if necessary.

George River is a pretty village, surrounded by hills, just on the tree line so nothing more than low shrubs grow. The house overlooks the bay. There are no motor vehicles here, only ski-doos and dog teams. Most of the dog teams are out at the moment but once all the snow has gone they will not be able to go out any more. Claude has very kindly lent me his camera so at least I have one. I was naturally very disappointed not to have my new Minolta camera by now. I have been down to look at the old nursing station which belongs to the federal government but is no longer used. I have decided that it is the ideal place to play my violin. No-one will be disturbed.

May 13th 1969

Claude's office doubles as administrator's office, post office, radio telephone office and my clinic. It is not a big office and I only have a little corner of it with a chair and a bookcase for the medicines. I share his desk for writing. Clinic hours are 1.30 till 4.30 p.m, which doesn't sound much but there will of course be home visits, immunisations, school visits and probably the occasional emergency from time to time. Claude has told me about the different clinics and Monday is apparently antenatal day. As Lorraine had no midwifery experience, she just asked about the mothers' last periods and took their word for it. I wanted to examine the mothers myself and make proper assessments so that I would know what to expect. In my experience so far it is not very helpful to ask when the last period was because Eskimos don't have much idea of time and it might have been the last full moon or the one before. I obviously could not carry out a proper antenatal clinic in Claude's office so France helped me set up a camp bed in the kitchen and this gave the women privacy and worked well. I found two Eskimos who will probably deliver soon. I understood that anyone who was likely to deliver during the break-up was to have already been sent to Chimo. Chatting to Carolyne later, who knows George River Eskimos very well, I learned that some mothers will not present themselves until the last minute because they don't want to spend two months away from home, which is understandable. I hope I get some deliveries! Finding equipment might be a problem. I shall have to look through all the stock.

France has a class of five-year-olds who she teaches here in the house, so I can borrow her interpreter if necessary. I don't have an interpreter myself.

George River: iceberg on shore

May 14th 1969

It was raining yesterday, which felt strange but it turned to snow in the night and we have had a snow storm today so there is definitely no hope of a plane now.

I did my first home visits today. Jessie, an old Eskimo lady, has a nasty leg ulcer which needs dressing three times a week. She lives in a one room shack, the smallest in the village apparently. Five people (I think) live there and they have recently bought a washing machine which just fits in among the three beds. I have managed to find and sterilise a few basic instruments in case I get a delivery, including some fishing line to tie off the cord; it is the only thing I could think of as it is clean and easy to sterilise. When our sister tutor used to ask us as student nurses, what we would do if we were ever in the bush and tell us, 'improvise!', I can remember thinking, 'well, I shan't ever end up in the bush.' But now I am and I'm already learning to improvise.

As well as all the posts in the Ungava Bay area: Fort Chimo, Wakeham Bay, Koartak, Payne Bay and Leaf Bay, we can hear radio telephone communications in posts along the Hudson Strait and Hudson Bay area: Sugluk, Povungnituk, Port Harrison and Great Whale River. Over time, names if not faces are going to become familiar. I have already had a chat to Louise in Wakeham Bay on the radio telephone. I am going to start 'Radio Ungava' and play the violin over the radio telephone. Of course it has to be after normal office hours and we have made a date so that Louise can be by the radio telephone in Wakeham Bay. That will be good fun.

May 15th 1969

All the dog teams are now back in the village after hunting. There are about 75 Huskies in all. I have been asked to vaccinate them against rabies. The person responsible has the vaccine but he has no experience and is reluctant to do it. So long as the dogs are held down I don't mind doing it. I didn't know I would be part-time vet as well! The last thing I need is an outbreak of rabies.

May 18th 1969

I gave Louise my first violin recital on 'Radio Ungava' yesterday evening! She and a few others were gathered round the radio telephone in Wakeham Bay. I had to find a way of holding down the 'speak' button with Sellotape. It was good fun and they apparently enjoyed it. Unfortunately Claude has told me today that it is not good for the radio telephone button to be held down for such a long time so Radio Ungava can no longer broadcast. A pity. At least we had one broadcast.

We actually had a plane at 7 p.m. on the 15th. That really will be the last now. I went out to it as I found three patients who needed to go to Chimo. The ice was better than the day I arrived, with a light covering of snow as a result of the snowstorm and the fact we haven't had any sun. So that the pilot would know where to land, the Eskimos made two lines of ski-doos on the ice. Johnny May was the pilot and he made a beautiful landing. Within minutes everything was loaded on to the komautiks and we were away again. I now have my full complement of underwear!

On Friday I started the immunisations (children, not dogs). I had the list which I was given in Chimo and decided to start with the schoolchildren. Luckily Carolyne was there to help me because my list of names, the French version, did not correspond with Carolyne's English version. As all Eskimos also have registration numbers at least we could identify them and I made up a new list. The children were very calm and it went very well. I will be able to do France's pre-school children at the house so that will leave just the remaining under-fives.

Yesterday (Saturday) I borrowed the school as a base for immunising the under-fives. Carolyne and Susie, her interpreter, had helped me broadcast my intention around the village on Friday evening and that I was planning to start at 2 p.m. At 2 p.m. there was not a soul in sight apart from Lucas, an Eskimo man, who apparently always helps hold the children. The village seemed totally silent until I learned that Tim, the other teacher, was giving out the welfare money. No wonder! I got a message sent over asking Tim to send parents and children to me after they had their money. About 20 minutes later a little boy of about 11 turned up with two toddlers in tow. He told me their names, waited while I gave them their immunisations and took them home. He kept coming back with various different children during the afternoon. A lot of toddlers were brought by their brothers or sisters. By 4 p.m. I had immunised 40 children which was more than I anticipated and there only remained 10 to do. So I was pleased with my afternoon's work. Having registration numbers and the names of the parents really helped me to be sure of having the right children. Another complication in George River is that more than half the population is called Annanak! There has been quite a bit of interbreeding here. Johnny also seems to be a recurring Christian name, I've noticed.

On Thursday a little boy of three and a half nearly drowned, falling through some snow into a lake. Luckily someone managed to get him out and they came to fetch me. I don't know how long he was in the water but he seemed to have recovered. I decided give him an injection of penicillin just in case.

The temperature has dropped down to the 20s again and there was another snow storm. The ice is harder than ever. The pilots will soon be taking the little planes south as they have to exchange the skis for floats. Little planes from Chimo to the outposts take off from Lake Stewart on floats in the summer.

May 22nd 1969

We had a fondue Bourgignonne with caribou meat the other night. It was absolutely delicious. Caribou live on moss and lichen and have a smelling gland in the foot, between the cloves, so they can smell food through the snow. Eskimos have always known this but whites did not believe it. More recently it has been proven. Nature is amazing! Caribou have been observed running and suddenly stopping dead in their tracks because they have smelled food under the snow.

Pasha Annanak wearing traditional caribou skin amauti

May 24th 1969

To our amazement there was another plane yesterday! We only heard about it just before it landed and Johnny May sent a message to say he had my new camera on board. I went out to the plane. Six Eskimos returned home from various hospitals. There had been 14 out and of those many were women, so a lot of women in the village have been looking after other people's children as well as their own. I asked Johnny jokingly if he wouldn't like to have a trip round over the village so I could finish my old film. "O.K," he said, "jump in. Anyone else?" So a few of us joined him and I managed to finish the film. It was a nice clear day too and Johnny flew low over the village, tipping the plane at different angles. The photos should be good.

May 26th 1969

I had run out of medicine bottles last week so Susie wrote out a notice to put up in the co-op, asking people to bring their empty bottles back. Only one bottle had appeared after two days so I had to think of something else. Susie and Carolyne kindly volunteered to go round all the houses and came back with 63 bottles, some of which went back several years. When we give out medicines we put the date as well as instructions on the labels.

On Sunday morning I went to church. The service is at ten o'clock and as only half a dozen Eskimos here have a clock or a watch and there may be a variation of up to two hours among them, no-one ever really knows the exact time. Elijah Emataluk is the lay minister and possesses a watch so everyone looks out of their window on a Sunday morning and when they see Elijah leave home, they know it is ten o'clock. (At least by Elijah's watch). The service was taken by Elijah and was just as restless as in Chimo but only lasted about an hour.

On Sunday afternoons here there is quite a routine, or perhaps it could even be called a ritual, of visiting. Everyone visits everyone else. In the afternoon I joined Carolyne and Susie to start the rounds. As it is such a small village, everyone sees everyone else most days. While the visiting is going on it is not uncommon to find one house completely empty (no locked doors here) or to find another house crammed with visitors! Visitors will sit awhile, maybe talking, maybe silent, invariably smoking and after awhile, I suppose when they feel they have been there long enough, will say "atai" (right) "taima" (finished), get up and go. We visited the Agnatuks first who live in a tent all the year round. He also has two wives which is unusual. Between the two wives, the children's ages range from three to thirty. The family has apparently been thrown out of some villages but they seem to be accepted here. The tent is quite roomy and has a stove in the middle made from an oil barrel cut in half with a cover over it. The chimney pipe goes through the roof of the tent.

Most houses are pretty primitive and apart from beds, which are mainly home-made, have no other furniture. Some beds have mattresses, others caribou skins or duvets filled with Canada Goose down, which the Eskimos have made themselves. People sit on beds or wooden boxes or trunks. Clothes are often hung on string across the room or piled into cardboard boxes, as I saw in Fort Chimo. Most are one-room shacks but one or two have government supplied prefabricated two-bedroom houses, shipped up in the summer. They all have little oil-fired stoves for heating. In the old days they would have used seal oil until the government started to supply coal. There is of course the prevailing smell of sealskin everywhere. Most houses have some kind of toilet utensil in the porch area, which they probably just empty outside. Susie's house is the only one I have seen with a proper little chemical toilet which is curtained off.

Susie is 22 and the oldest of eight children; the youngest is three. Her father was accidentally shot in the back three years ago; he is paralysed and permanently in hospital down south. The family goes to visit him once a year. What a tragedy for them!

May 29th 1969

I have been busy giving the schoolchildren medical examinations, from top to toe and have found a lot of impetigo, lice, enlarged tonsils and a couple of children with irregular heartbeats. I have now finished Carolyne's class of 26 six to ten-year-olds. Tim's class with the older ones, will be more difficult I suspect, as they will be embarrassed and self-conscious. The younger ones are quite uninhibited.

Yesterday there was an emergency: thirteen-month-old baby Silassie fell off a bed and as he turned blue and stopped breathing, the family thought he was dead. They came running to fetch me. I found him conscious but not very responsive. There was no way of knowing if he had a fractured skull so it was a question of close observation. In Fort Chimo of course, he would have been admitted to hospital. As I wanted to check on him hourly I thought I might take him into the house with me for the night and sleep downstairs with him. I obviously couldn't have him in Véronique's room. Claude was not happy about this so I had to think of something else. This was a family where the mother was away and an aunt was looking after her children as well as her own but the aunt doesn't sleep there as the father is home at night. As Eskimos sleep so deeply I couldn't rely on anyone waking every hour to check on the baby anyway so I decided I would have to spend the night there. I took my duvet and atigi and prepared to sleep on the floor of this very dirty house. The family was very grateful; the aunt was so worried, especially as it was not her baby. Nobody noticed that I woke Silassie every hour and changed him a couple of times. I slept a little in between times. Two of the older children I noticed, spent a good part of the night scratching in their sleep. (Head lice thrive in this environment). By the morning Silassie seemed full of beans, babbling happily, so I went back to the house and had a very welcome hot bath.

June 1st 1969

After the incident with Baby Silassie, I decided I would like to move into the old nursing station. I had also gathered that the Eskimos didn't like having to come up to the house with their problems because of the lack of privacy and in fact have been seeking me out in the village anyway or asking me to visit them.

The nursing station is a short-stay cabin of the DEW Line style, painted white. As far as I know, it has never been lived in for more than a few days. It is right on the edge of the village, overlooking the bay. Being the first building to be seen from the water there is a permanently revolving light on the roof. The light has long since ceased to function but it continues to revolve, over my bedroom. I expect I will get used to it. There is a chemical toilet in the porch area, a sink in the main room, though needless to say, no running water or drainage so I have put a bucket under the sink and will have to remember to empty it before it overflows. A clean 45 gallon oil drum contains my week's supply of water. There is an oil stove for heating and cooking. Because the two smaller rooms are just partitioned off from the main room the heat can circulate everywhere. One of these small rooms is my bedroom and I have made the other into my 'surgery'. There is also electricity. Carolyne has lent me some curtains, a rug and a tablecloth. She is going to get her schoolchildren to do some paintings for me to put on the walls so that will be fun. There is already a supply of pans, crockery and cutlery here. I have had to patch up some of the broken windows with polythene.

After school on Friday all the schoolchildren helped me carry the medicines down to the nursing station. Many hands made light work! Cough syrup, cod liver oil, iron tonic and diarrhoea mixture come in half-gallon bottles of which there is a good supply. Most medicines come by sea on the annual ship in the summer. They have to be ordered annually because air freight is very expensive: it costs a dollar per pound weight. Vaccines can be flown in.

George River: Elijah Emataluk (Anglican minister) and wife Kitty

June 2nd 1969

I love my little house on the hill! I keep a bucket of water on the stove so I have a constant hot water supply. Oil consumption seems quite good: one and a half inches in 12 hours. (11 inches is about four gallons). If I run out of oil I will have to move back to the house, so it's in my own interest to be economical. Tim and Carolyne came over with a bottle of wine and we drank to this new venture.

June 6th 1969

The ice on the bay is now broken up but the bay is still very clogged up. The ice seems to take a long time to move away. At every incoming tide we have a new selection of icebergs coming in and being left behind on the beach when the tide goes out again. When the ice cracks it sounds like blasting, echoing across the bay. Every day we walk along the mountainside to watch progress. Some Eskimos set out with six canoes three days ago, heading for Fort Chimo but couldn't get past the ice and arrived back here in the early hours this morning. The weather is sunny and perfect for walking. I manage to have a walk every day.

This afternoon we organised the Husky vaccinating. Carolyne volunteered to help me. We dissolved all the vaccines at her house and then set off in two teams. I started at one end of the village and Carolyne at the other. We had plenty of Eskimos to hold the dogs. I must have looked like the Pied Piper with the following of children across the village. I had done about 40 dogs when I met up with Carolyne's team which made a total of 65 in all. It all went very well and was also good fun.

June 9th 1969

We have had several inches of snow today. The weather is quite unpredictable.

The schoolchildren have done some wonderful paintings and drawings for me. Most of them feature ski-doos, dog teams or planes but a few have done brightly coloured flowers. The detail in some is extraordinary. I put them up on my walls and the children have been over to see them. I think they are proud of their work.

I had a message from Quebec asking if I would be willing to stay here until August. I am absolutely delighted, overjoyed, as I am so happy here and really feel part of the village already. I would love to stay a year but I don't think that will happen. I know that if Fort Chimo becomes short-staffed, someone is taken out of one of the small posts to return to Chimo. There is always that insecurity. I have actually been making enquiries about working for the Federal Government. Eileen has worked for them and says they are more organised. Bernard has contacted Montreal on his DOT radio on my behalf and they have offered me a post when the break-up is over. I really don't want to go back to Chimo again. With the federal government, I would be working in one of the settlements along the Hudson Bay coast: Great Whale River, Port Harrison, Povungnituk or Sugluk on the Hudson Strait. I don't really want to work in Great Whale River because it is even bigger than Chimo although there is no hospital there. I love working in a small village.

June 12th 1969

Four canoes actually managed to get to Chimo and returned here yesterday. There was great excitement and everyone went down to meet them on the beach. They had brought provisions from Chimo as well as news of George River Eskimos out at the moment. The bay is now open here but of course we have to wait for Lake Stewart in Fort Chimo, to be clear before planes can come in as they have to take off with floats.

Very soon I shall be the only white woman here as Carolyne and Tim will be on holiday and Claude and France will be leaving on the first plane, not coming back. I don't know what the mechanic's plans are, I never see him.

George River has only had formal education for five years so the 11 and 12-year-olds speak the best English. Adults who speak fluent English are those who had to spend years in TB sanatoria when they were younger. TB is still quite a problem here and all the Eskimos have to have annual chest X-rays.

I love going into the school, the children are so responsive. Tim plays the guitar and sings; we often play music together. He has taught his class many English songs which they love. I have taught them *'Dashing Away with the Smoothing Iron'* and they caught on really fast. I have heard one or two of them humming it to themselves around the village. I am planning to do some First Aid with Tim's class next week. I often go to the school at lunch times, to do the head lice treatments. At least there is running water there.

I am beginning to understand and speak more Inuktituk (Eskimo). 'Imaha' is one of the most recurring words in the Arctic, it means 'maybe'. Nothing is ever certain here! It reminds me a bit of Spain's 'mañana' (tomorrow)! Another word which is interesting is 'anurak' which means 'clothing'. I wonder whether our word 'anorak' has come down to us via the Greenland Eskimos to Scandinavia. 'Igloo' means 'house', or 'dwelling', not just 'ice house'. There are many words for snow, depending on what kind it is or whether it is falling or already on the ground. 'Aputi' is snow on the ground. There are also two words for water: 'imak' is 'sweet water' or 'fresh water', 'tareuk' is 'sea water'. Language has always fascinated me, I love to try and see connections. Although I don't have an interpreter myself, Susie helps me when she can. Adult patients are often accompanied by a child who speaks English and of course, my Inuktituk is improving all the time!

George River: fishing

June 17th 1969

Summer is really in the air now and everyone seems to go out fishing whenever they can. High tide is the best time for fishing apparently. A lot of the Eskimos have gone out to their summer camps already where they live in tents and spend the summer fishing. Many of them are on an island about 12 miles away. I hope to get a chance to visit there. The George River is rich in Arctic char which is rather like a cross between salmon and trout. Absolutely delicious. There is no need to use bait, the fish just go for the hook. Many Eskimos just throw out a hook on a bit of line wound round a stone or stick. Tim lent me his fishing rod but I managed to get it all tangled up so I resorted to 'Eskimo style' and immediately caught a fish. They aren't very big, usually two to four pounds. Mine was about three pounds. I have ordered a spin-casting reel from the Bay in Chimo. Tim has shown me how to degut a fish, down by the water so I can take it home already cleaned. Nothing is more delicious than fresh fish cooked within minutes of catching it. I have tasted quite a variety of local produce this week: char, caribou, seagull's egg and wild goose.

What I thought was a disaster has turned out to be a wonderful experience. Last week I broke my watch. Now I don't have any reason to be tied down to time. I can live like the

Eskimos: eat when I'm hungry, sleep when I'm tired etc. Of course one is aware of morning, noon and night even though it doesn't get really dark at night at all. I soon stopped clinic hours when I moved to the nursing station, as I used to sit waiting for patients in the afternoons and no-one came. They didn't know what the time was anyway. The village is so small that everyone knows where I am and they just tend to come and find me if they need me. It's a much better arrangement. Even when I put a note 'gone fishing' on my door they will find me down by the river.

June 27th 1969

In July and August American tourists stay on the island and pay 90 dollars a day for guaranteed fishing. The island was originally a Hudson's Bay trading post which Willy Emudluk, an Eskimo man, ran single-handed. When it ceased to be a trading post Willy started up the tourist business and the Lodge where the tourists stay, is called Ilkalu Lodge. (Ilkalu is Inuktituk for fish). A French Canadian couple, Madeleine and John Ardello, come up for those two months, to cook and cater for the tourists.

A couple of days ago some Eskimos came from the island to ask me to visit old Lucy who has a bad heart. I suspected she had run out of medicine. We set off in a canoe (all canoes here have outboard motors) to the island. As I thought, Lucy had run out of medicine so I gave her a new supply. While I was there I decided to immunise the children I had missed. I spent the afternoon fishing but didn't catch anything so walked along the rocks and watched children playing in the rock pools. Even the three-year-olds seem to keep up with the older children. What a wonderful life for them! Some of the Eskimos are busy getting the Lodge ready for the first tourists who are due next week. Willy Emudluk and two others had gone to Chimo to fetch Madeleine and John and bring them to the Lodge for the summer. Selina Emudluk, (Willy's wife) looked after me and took me to her tent. She kept feeding me on tea and Bannock, a kind of scone bread which is what they seem to eat most of the time.

Others were just coming in and helping themselves but I didn't like to do that. Selina made sure I didn't starve. As I couldn't leave again until high tide (about 4 a.m.), I was given a place on a bed and Selina gave me a towel to cover me. There were 11 of us in the tent altogether, with three beds. I think I was sharing with an uncle. No-one got undressed to sleep, they just covered themselves with something. There was a communal pot in the middle of the floor and one by one everyone relieved themselves before emptying the pot outside. I had already 'been' behind a rock so didn't have to suffer any embarrassment until later in the night, by which time everyone was asleep anyway. Peter and Joshua came to wake me about 4 a.m. to take me back on the high tide. It was a beautiful morning, the water was black and smooth, the sun shining through the clouds. I was so glad to have been able to see how they were living on the island, just as they used to live in the old days. It was really cosy in the tent too.

Today is the last day of term so Carolyne and Tim will be leaving next week. I shall miss them both. Claude and family are also leaving for good. Planes are back in Chimo now, ready with their floats, so we might get a plane tomorrow.

I haven't mentioned much about the different medical conditions I have dealt with since I have been here but now, going through my records it is quite a list: half the population have or have had TB, one near drowning, one possible fractured skull, one fractured clavicle, strained muscles, bronchitis, otitis, colds, flu, toothache, cuts and bruises, abscesses, impetigo, cystitis, constipation, stomach troubles, warts, high blood pressure, heart problems, conjunctivitis and pregnancy.

July 1st 1969

We had our first plane on June 28th so the break-up only lasted just over a month. I had several letters from home which was lovely. I must say I did miss getting letters. My new spin-cast fishing rod also arrived.

Yesterday we had another plane and I had three patients to send out. It was low tide, which meant a long walk along the mud flats to get to the water. We waited on some rocks until the plane landed and then got into a canoe to reach the plane. Floats are much bulkier than skis which makes the door into the plane much higher. The pilot let a ladder down into the canoe and people climbed up into the plane. Carolyne also went out on that plane so I am now the only white woman in the village. Tim is still here. Donald, a law student, is the temporary administrator for the summer, replacing Claude. He seems very confident.

I was just having a meal with Tim this evening when I was interrupted for Lizzie, a two-and-a-half year old who had fallen off a swing and cut her eyelid. I was thankful this was not my first case of suturing. It was such a delicate place. Two people held Lizzie firmly while I worked as quickly as possible. Fortunately the eye itself was not injured. Back to Tim's for dessert and five minutes later another call! This time there was a panic about one of my pregnant women. Her house was full of people and I presumed she was in premature labour. It turned out she was suffering from shock as there had been a fire in the house and she was alone with the children. Nobody could explain exactly what had happened but as the house was still full of smoke I advised her to go and sleep somewhere else for the night. Whatever the fire was, it had now gone out. She was just very frightened. Later that evening we went down to see any boats that were leaving (all comings and goings attract attention). Suddenly a two-year-old fell in the water! I rushed to the water's edge just as he crawled out on his own. He was unscathed apart from being very wet.

July 7th 1969

I removed Lizzie's stitches yesterday. She had to be held again while I removed them. The eyelid has healed beautifully so I'm very pleased.

Tim was supposed to be leaving today but it has been stormy and foggy. There was a layer of snow on the mountains this morning! So we will have another evening together playing music and scrabble. I was trying to catch up with my paperwork earlier when Susie came running up to the nursing station to tell me Levina was in labour. She had another six weeks to go so now I was going to have a premature baby on my hands. I grabbed the equipment I had sterilised a few weeks ago and followed Susie to the house. Levina was settled on a caribou skin on the floor and several women were there to support her. I examined her and found she was definitely in labour but after a while it seemed to stop. The women came and went, sat and smoked so there was always someone for support. When it was clear that labour had stopped, I radioed Chimo and asked for a plane. They said they would send one at 7.30 p.m. Susie had stayed with us during these hours and she managed to get hold of some men to carry Levina on a stretcher down to the plane. The tide was out the furthest possible so we had a two mile walk across the mud flats. The stretcher was home-made and rather heavy, even more so with a pregnant woman. Levina was very calm. It wasn't cold despite the rain. No sign of the plane when we got down there so we just waited, having put the stretcher down on some rocks. As no-one, including myself, goes far without their fishing rods, we passed the time fishing. Suddenly Donald, our temporary administrator, came running down having had a radio message from Chimo to say that the plane hadn't left yet but that a doctor would be on board. I was relieved about that because I didn't want to have to go to Chimo. The new doctor, whom I hadn't met, finally arrived with two nurses. They had come to do some immunisations! I explained that I had done them all already. I was rather annoyed, as they should have known this from my reports. By the end of the day I was somewhat exhausted.

George River: Johnny Etok and Sammy

July 12th 1969

Tim finally left on the 10th so we had a lot of 'last games of scrabble'. I really miss him now. We had become very close.

On the 11th I had a difficult situation with the family of a woman I was sending out to hospital on the next plane. The family was panicking, believing her to be dangerously ill and demanded that she be flown out immediately. I tried to reassure them that she was not dangerously ill but they sent for Stanley Annanak, the Eskimo chief, and told him I was not doing my job properly, which was very nerve-wracking. He turned up at my place with his interpreter and I discussed the situation with him. He seemed to understand but under the circumstances I thought perhaps it would be better if I did get a plane for the woman straightaway, which I did. This is the only time I have had problems with demanding Eskimos so it shook me up a bit. Susie is very supportive and I gather this is not the first time there have been problems with this family. All is now calm anyway.

I am living on fish! I am very happy with this diet of fish and Bannock. I have become so addicted I don't know how I'll cope without it when I leave here. I go out fishing most days but I have a good supply in the village freezer for days when I'm too busy. It seems incongruous to have a freezer in the Arctic. As the Eskimos export Arctic char down south they have to keep it frozen in the meantime. It is a good source of income for them. I have my own little corner in this walk-in freezer.

The Eskimos are still living off the land (and water) here. They are very enterprising. Because George River is just above the tree line, once a year the Eskimos take out their canoes and head south to go logging. After a few days they return with the logs trailing behind the canoes. They have their own saw mill in the village and are lucky to have some wood for building. I heard a wonderful anecdote recently: someone was trying to explain how precious wood is in the Arctic and added, "...after all it doesn't grow on trees!" Another interesting thing about the Eskimos in George River is that they have no alcohol in the village. They are proud not to drink. I don't think they object to whites drinking though. I have only heard of one Eskimo who was given whisky by a white man and was so drunk he fell asleep with a lighted cigarette. He woke later to find his bed on fire. He was so ashamed he didn't even come to see me with his burns. I just hope he wasn't severely burned. I don't know who it was.

I have handed in my notice and plan to leave, weather permitting of course, August 6th. I shall go to Montreal and meet my new supervisor, Ora Babcock. Eileen knows Ora and says she is very nice and good fun. I have spoken to Eileen on the radio telephone. Carolyne also knows Ora and told me a very amusing incident: a few years ago, one summer, when Carolyne was a student, she did some voluntary work in the Arctic working with Ora. Ora was doing a medical survey in Eskimo settlements and they needed to obtain urine specimens. Ora and Carolyne went into a tent and tried to explain to the women there what they wanted. They could not get the message across no matter how hard they tried! Eventually, Ora gave quite a graphic demonstration. At last the Eskimos showed signs of enlightenment, of having understood and with one accord left the tent so that Ora could have some privacy alone in the tent!

I shall be based somewhere in the Hudson Bay area after I have been to Montreal. Although I am absolutely loving it here and shall be sad to leave, I know it can't last for ever. I could be taken back to Chimo, without warning, at any time.

July 14th 1969

The village is quite deserted now that most families have gone out to their summer camps. I went fishing with Susie's 12-year-old sister Jessie on Saturday and caught five fish. Yesterday Johnny Morgan came to invite me to go out in his canoe with him and Donald. We went out on the high tide, fished for a bit and then went over to the island. I went round to say 'hello' to everyone which was lovely. They all seemed pleased to see me. These Eskimos are so friendly. I learned that Bobby Baron had gone to the village to see me so we just missed each other. I went to meet Madeleine Ardello at the Lodge. She and her husband John have been coming up here for years every summer. It was nice to speak to another white woman for a change! I had a cup of coffee there. There are no tourists at the moment.

The Island: the Emudluks' tent where I spent a night

July 15th 1969

Johnny Etok and Johnny Nagolak came to fetch me this morning from the island, as there are several people sick with flu. Johnny Nagolak is a real character and plays the accordion. When he learned that I was twenty-nine he couldn't believe it and has been calling me 'twenty-nine horse power' ever since! He has also made me a lovely stone carving of a polar bear, with even the little foot pads in detail.

There was great excitement when we got to the island as they had caught a caribou and were busy cutting it up by the water's edge. Apparently Johnny May had just taken off from the island in his plane, when he spotted the caribou and flew back to the island to tell the islanders where it was. They managed to drag it back behind a canoe. I went round my patients and found a few with infected mosquito bites as well as people with flu. Temperatures have been in the 70s and 80s this week but because of the mosquitoes we still have to keep arms and legs covered up. We walk around with cans of 'Off' spray but it doesn't seem to last more than a couple of minutes. The other night I had mosquitoes in my bed and they were driving me crazy. I couldn't understand it until the next day when I examined my windows and found a tiny hole in one of the polythene patches. I am still scratching now. Just one tiny hole can cause so much misery! I spray DDT around the place before I go to bed and my first job in the morning is sweeping up dead flies which are also in abundance.

Johnny Morgan and Lucas Etok apparently caught two seals yesterday but lost one. As the seals are not so fat in the summer, they don't float for long after being shot so hunters have to be very quick to catch them before they sink.

We haven't had a mail plane for about ten days. I am anxiously awaiting my first Minolta slides.

July 22nd 1969

I was called out to the island again for the third time last week and Susie came out with me. We planned to come back on the same tide but by the time we had been round doling out aspirin and cough syrup, the wind had got up and it was too rough to leave so we prepared to spend the night there. Four boys from the Belcher Islands visiting the island, had gone fishing up the Korak River for a couple of days, so we borrowed their tent for the night. We went over to the Lodge and had a chat with Madeleine. The only tourist was also fishing up the Korak River so we didn't meet him. Someone lent us a sleeping bag and we lit a fire in the tent so we were quite cosy. Susie helped herself to their soap, towels and toothpaste so I followed suit. It doesn't do to be squeamish! Actually, George River Eskimos are quite clean. Not many leave meat around on the floor now, as they did in the past.

The wind persisted for two days so we had a real little holiday once the sick visiting was done. We had some lovely walks round the island and Madeleine fed us very well. I had been living off Char and Bannock for weeks so it was a treat.

I can now understand much more Eskimo and Susie has been helping me. I have a vocabulary of about a hundred words or phrases.

We managed to get back to the village on Sunday. It now looks as if the flu epidemic is starting here.

July 26th 1969

The day after we returned to the village I heard that some porcupines had attacked some dogs or the dogs attacked the porcupines, I'm not sure which. In any case, there had been an encounter. One dog was killed and another had a face full of quills. Johnny Jake, the owner of the dogs, came to ask if I could do anything. I offered to give the dog a tranquilliser so that Johnny would be able to approach closer. The dog was naturally ferocious as it hadn't been able to eat or drink as well as being in pain, I suppose. Despite this, Johnny managed to hold the dog while I gave the injection. We waited for this to take effect and when the dog seemed calmer, two Eskimos held the dog still with a rope round its neck and Johnny and I set to pulling out the quills with pliers. The quills were about three inches long, one inch of which was embedded. After about ten minutes of quill pulling, we noticed that the dog seemed unnaturally still, in fact on closer examination, was dead. The Eskimos had been pulling too tight on the rope. This was rather sad after all our efforts but as the dog also had quills inside the mouth I don't think it would have survived. I know that my courage would have failed when it came to reaching inside the mouth. I was rather upset but Johnny was grateful for my having tried to help. Eskimos have a theory that seal oil poured over the quills helps them fall out but this takes time. With the heat and lack of fluids it was unlikely that the dog would have lived long enough.

Salmon have now come to the river. I went fishing with Jessie, Susie's twelve-year-old sister, yesterday and she caught a huge salmon. She was so frightened she gave me her rod for me to bring it in. I was frightened of this monster myself and had no idea how I was going to deal with it. It was leaping in and out of the water. When the line broke, I was really quite relieved. Then I got one on my line and the same thing happened again. No wonder little Jessie was so scared. We went back to the village to find Conlucy and Bobby looking for me from the island. More flu. I went back with them, visited the patients, had supper at the Lodge and came straight home despite the rough water. Willy Etok, being a skillful boat man, brought me safely back. It was a rather bumpy ride.

The Island: children

July 29th 1969

We actually had a mail plane yesterday. I had five letters from home and my first Minolta film is back; I'm absolutely thrilled with the results. The slides are all excellent.

Now my time in George River is coming to an end I'm going to find it really hard to be back in civilisation again. It has been wonderful to experience living like the Eskimos; a blissfully stress-free existence, not having to worry about time, going fishing when I wanted and eating 'Eskimo style'. Even having to manage on 45 gallons of water a week was a challenge. At first I was so economical, I had about a third left. Then, I went the other way and ran out. One week they forgot to bring me any water and I had to fetch it by the bucketful myself from the river. I now have it down to a fine art. Having long hair, I can only wash it alternate weeks and wash clothes in the other. It is not possible to wash both hair and clothes in the same week. My biggest problem has been to remember to empty the bucket under the sink before it overflows. It has also been an amazing outdoor life, which I love. The freeze-up will be quite different I think. It is hard to believe I have only been in the Arctic for five months. Although my time here is coming to an end and I'm sad about that, a new chapter is just about to begin.

There was a fantastic full moon yesterday! Not only was it full but the tide was high with the huge yellow moon reflected in the water. I was able to take some photos of the moon and reflection, just standing outside my house. An hour later the moon was too high to capture both moon and reflection together.

They are expecting a hundred tourists at Ilkalu Lodge in August. To think, the tourists pay $90 a day for being here and I get paid $400 a month for being here!

Having not had any worldwide news for months, anything could be happening. Madeleine or John told me the other day that someone has just landed on the moon. I wonder if they were up there when I was taking photos of it.

July 31st 1969

Yesterday was a hot, close day and the mosquitoes were terrible. Susie's 18-year-old sister Maggie and I went for a walk along the mountainside to look for flowers. I have been collecting and pressing flowers and become very enthusiastic. I have quite a few species already. They are of course tiny, stunted because of the climate but nevertheless pretty. The summer season is also very short. August is about the only snow-free month here it seems. It is also the season of blueberries. Blueberries are apparently so rich in vitamin C that it can be stored in the body for six months. This is very interesting, as people have wondered over the years how the Eskimos obtained their vitamins as no other fruit or vegetables grow here and they don't like tinned ones either. Originally Eskimos also used to eat part of the contents of the caribou stomach which contained vitamins from moss and lichen. Not all the blueberries will be eaten before the snow comes so the rest will be uncovered when the snow melts in the spring (deep freeze!) which means another six month's supply of vitamin C. Of course they also get plenty of other vitamins from fish oils. Seal liver has the highest iron content of all livers apparently and I find it delicious. I wasn't too keen on polar bear meat, which I tried. It tasted like tough stewing steak with a fishy flavour.

When Maggie and I got back from our walk, we decided to go and visit old Elisie, Maggie's grandmother. She is seventy and a great character, always laughing and full of fun. We got her talking about the old days and unlike many of the older people, she was happy to do so. Her father died of starvation and Elisie remembers people eating dogs in times of starvation; she doesn't remember anyone eating people. Elisie wouldn't eat dog, she told us. When she told us that her grandfather had three wives, we were fascinated. This was also news to Maggie! But Elisie went on to explain that it wasn't three at once, the first two died.

Supplies are running low here and in Chimo apparently. We have no more meat or eggs, the co-op has run out of hooks and lines, matches and cigarette papers. People are splitting cardboard to roll cigarettes. I found some ancient jellies in a cupboard; and although they wouldn't 'jell', the result made a refreshing drink. I also found some dehydrated egg powder but it was revolting. As long as I have fish and flour to make Bannock, I am happy. The annual supply ships will be coming some time in August.

This morning I was called out to Annie Annanak who was in labour. I was a bit worried as she had not had a very good pregnancy and wasn't due for another three or four weeks. She was already settled on her caribou skin on the floor with several women to support her and her husband Johnny was sitting there faithfully holding her hand. After a couple of hours she delivered a lovely baby boy so I was delighted. I tied the cord off with my pre-sterilised fishing line which worked well. I weighed the baby on the post office scales and he weighed 5lbs 4oz. I am overjoyed to have been able to bring at least one little George River baby into the world.

August 1st 1969

I was woken in the early hours this morning for Susie Morgan in labour. I had been expecting this any day and was not surprised. I always wanted to deliver her as it was her third pregnancy, which has been very straightforward so I was thrilled. She was settled on her caribou skin with the usual gathering of support and in a short time the baby appeared. Another beautiful boy who weighed in at 7lbs 13½ozs on the accurate post office scales. Her two other children aged two and three and a half, slept through all this but little Mae (three and a half) woke later wide-eyed and wondering to find another little brother on the bed. There may not be much mail to weigh but the scales have been put to good use this week. Now I have brought two little George River babies into the world!

August 4th 1969

We had a plane a couple of days ago and a new temporary doctor and his wife were on board. They came to see the settlement, the new babies and do the immunisations (!!) (My patience is running out!) I wasn't expecting them but fortunately Donald was. They wanted a meal as soon as they arrived and luckily Donald had some 'civilised' food otherwise I would have served them fish and Bannock, 'Eskimo style'. I knew that the mechanic had wanted to see a doctor so I told them this and said I would go and fetch him. "Why don't you phone him?" asked the doctor's wife. My mouth must have fallen open as I had forgotten such possibilities existed. When I explained that we didn't have phones here it was her turn to be surprised. "What do you do if someone needs you at night?" she asked. "They just come and get me". I told her. No running water was another impossible concept for her. The doctor wanted to know if there were other pregnant women and when their last periods were! I don't know what sort of impressions they took away with them that evening, they seemed rather shocked by it all.

Some fresh meat arrived with the plane and I had some veal. I ate half a pound of it with no trouble at all, having not tasted meat, apart from occasional corned beef, for weeks. I know that I am used to eating two pounds of fish regularly, it is so delicious a few hours after catching it.

August 5th 1969

I am having a busy week this week, what with the new mothers and babies, (all doing well). Some of the patients with heart problems are being affected by the heat and tend to get a bit panicky, thinking their time has come. I also have lovely baby Pasha with me in the nursing station; she is a year old and I suspect has meningitis. I need to get her to hospital. I am nursing her in the dark and have a notice: 'quiet please' on the door. We are supposed to be getting a plane today and there is a dentist on board too who will stay a few days so I am trying to get the message around to everyone here and on the island. He will be a welcome visitor I suspect. The village freezer has broken down which will be a major disaster if the Eskimos lose all that fish and income. I have put my little collection in Donald's freezer at the house. The Eskimos are hoping to get all the fish on a plane and it could still be saved if the freezer can't be repaired in time. I do hope the fish will be saved as the Eskimos all work so hard to be self-sufficient. I have been too busy to go fishing lately.

August 6th 1969

What confusion yesterday! Having got everyone over from the island who wanted to see the dentist, I was told that the plane was going to the island first. When the plane finally turned up, there was no dentist on board. I was anxious to get Pasha to hospital as well. A second plane had landed on the island so I contacted the island to let them know I was bringing the sick baby over. Noah very kindly said he would take me over there in his canoe and Pasha's mother came too. Noah's canoe was already down at the water's edge. By the time we walked down to the water it started to rain so we grabbed some extra clothes from another boat down there and set off for the island. Noah's canoe then started leaking 'too much' so we decided to abandon it and borrow the big boat from which we had borrowed the extra clothes. This boat belonged to a family who had arrived from Nain, Labrador a few weeks ago. It was really sluggish to start and finally when it did, it only moved at a snail's pace. It must have been quite a journey from Labrador! After about half an hour chugging along at this pace, we met someone in a canoe coming over from the island and we were informed that the plane had already left and wasn't going to Chimo anyway. By the time we got back to George River we must have been away about three hours. This was not the recommended treatment for meningitis but luckily Pasha wasn't any worse for the outing. I radioed the doctor and he said he would send a plane in the following morning (this morning). I kept Pasha with me all night, she is very poorly. She is such a beautiful baby, it is sad to see her so ill. Her temperature has come down though so that is something. Susie has been here quite a lot and Pasha's mother will sit with the baby later. It is raining and foggy so I doubt we will get a plane today. Poor John, from the Lodge, is suffering with a dental abscess and staying in Tim's old house, waiting for the dentist.

August 12th 1969
FORT CHIMO

I'm now back in Fort Chimo! My time in George River came to an abrupt end on Saturday (9th).

On August 6th I left Pasha's mother in charge while I went out to do all my visits and came back to find the mother fast asleep! She didn't even wake when I came in, washed some nappies and knocked the coffee pot over. It's a good job I was looking after Pasha at night. The plane finally arrived that evening about 6 p.m. and a nurse from Chimo came to fetch Pasha. I must say I was very relieved. The dentist arrived, stayed a few days and there were extractions all round; people were walking around with their mouths stuffed with Kleenex for a couple of days.

They caught a white whale at the island the other day and sent me some over. It was delicious, with a texture like tripe but with a fishy flavour. I was hoping for some more but I was whisked away before they could get it to me. Today was supposed to have been my leaving day but on Friday (the 10th) I heard at 10 p.m. that they were sending a plane in the next morning, to fetch the mechanic, the dentist and me. What a shock! I didn't want the end to be so sudden. Although I had already sent in my notice for August 6th, somewhere, deep down, I was hoping they would forget I was there. I felt I wanted to stay for ever. I went to Susie's house, very upset, to tell her. I stayed with them for awhile and Maggie came back with me to keep me company while I packed. When she had gone I wrote my records up to date and a report for my successor. I eventually managed a couple of hours sleep before getting up to fit in as many visits as I could before the plane arrived. I wanted to say 'goodbye' to as many people as possible and top up supplies of medicines for patients and vitamins for all the pregnant women, not knowing when the next nurse might come in. A new pregnant woman presented herself to me saying she thought she was eight or nine months pregnant! A quick examination proved her to be 36 weeks so I gave her some vitamins and added her name to my antenatal list for the next nurse and for Chimo. The plane was 'possibly 11 o'clock'. I was sad not to have been able to go over to the island and see everyone for the last time. I managed to radio them and I think if fuel for the motors hadn't been in short supply, some of them might have come out to the plane. Had Johnny May been the pilot he would have certainly taken me to the island before going on to Chimo, but he wasn't. At 12 p.m. Susie came down with me in a canoe to the plane, at least, to the floating dock. We were left on the floating dock with all my luggage. It was about an hour and a half later that the single-engine Norseman appeared overhead. I was really glad Susie had been with me all that time. I was in tears boarding the plane that was to remove me from that beautiful place and lovely people who had accepted me as one of their own.

45 minutes later I was back in Chimo (civilisation)! Louise, who had returned from Wakeham Bay four days previously, was there to meet me! That was a wonderful surprise and a comfort. I immediately felt better seeing her and we had so much to catch up on and compare notes. She really understood what it was like to have been so close to the Eskimos in a small settlement. It was the same for her in Wakeham Bay.

I have been to see Eileen and Bernard; their new baby is now six weeks old.

It feels really strange to see so many white people around! They all look the same to me. I can now understand how we appear to people of other races. Having only seen Eskimos for such a long time, I now see whites as they do. After those weeks in George River I could see that the Eskimos looked quite different from each other and I could even recognise different family characteristics.

Louise and I are both flying to Montreal tonight, taking two babies with us: Pasha and Charlotte, both George River babies. Pasha is much better but needs further investigations in hospital. I hope she hasn't got TB meningitis.

August 13th 1969
MONTREAL

We arrived in Montreal at 11 p.m. on Tuesday night and Louisette was there to meet us with her car. It was good to see her again but sad to hear that her sister had died of Hodgkin's disease. The two babies were going to Quebec but I would be returning to Montreal afterwards. However, as Pasha had started convulsing on the descent in the plane, I made the decision to take her to St Justine's hospital in Montreal. I didn't want a repeat of the last trip to Quebec, although it would have been quite different with Louisette driving of course, but Quebec was too far to take a convulsing baby. So we said our 'goodbyes' and I took a taxi to the hospital, leaving Pasha in what I hoped was the best care. I phoned Madame B for the last time, to tell her where Pasha was.

Today I have phoned to arrange my interview with the federal government for tomorrow afternoon.

This is the end of one era and another is about to begin.

George River:Noah with a seal

CHAPTER 3
GREAT WHALE RIVER

August 17th 1969

On Thursday the 14th I went for my interview at the federal government headquarters in Montreal. Mlle Pauline Laurin is the director of nursing services, Northern Health Services and is an extraordinary person. When she was a student nurse, her brother was a bush pilot in the Hudson Bay area and occasionally she would fly up with him to these Eskimo settlements. She was fascinated but also saw how much in need of health services they were. At that time there were only missionaries and Hudson's Bay Company traders up there. Once she was qualified she started to set up health services in the Hudson Bay area. She is one of the most dynamic people I have ever met and she inspires others with her enthusiasm, she is so dedicated. To my surprise, she seems to think I have a lot of Arctic experience already, after only five months.

I am to go to Sugluk, which is a little settlement of about 350 Eskimos and about 15 white people. It is the furthest north of all the Hudson Bay area settlements, on the Hudson Strait. (1500 miles from H.Q. in Montreal). Apparently the village is even more beautiful than George River; it is surrounded by mountains and the entrance to the village from the Hudson Strait is like a fjord. The health centre is another DEW Line type hut like George River and my residence is a 50 foot trailer with all mod cons. I also get a ski-doo and I shall have an interpreter as well as a cleaning lady. I wasn't sure I wanted a cleaning lady but Mlle Laurin has made it clear that the nurses must save their energy for nursing, not cleaning! $50 a month will be taken off my salary for board and lodging but I can spend as much as I like on food and soft drinks, without worrying about the cost and the bill just goes to Montreal.

While I am in Sugluk I shall also be responsible for Ivujivik, a very small settlement on the north-west tip of Quebec where the Hudson Bay and the Hudson Strait meet. As there are only about 110 Eskimos there, it is too small for a permanent nurse. Steve, who is a teacher, is the lay dispenser in Ivujivik and has had some basic health training. When he has problems, he will contact me on the radio telephone. I shall be able to visit twice a year to do immunisations, health checks and chest X-rays.

On the way to Sugluk I am to spend a week in Great Whale River where Ora Babcock, the zone nursing officer, will meet me and then she will go up to Sugluk with me for a week to give me some orientation. I am to leave for Great Whale River on August 27th. Mlle Laurin said Ora and I will get on very well together.

The temperatures in Montreal are in the 90s! It's unbearable. I can't wait for the 27th! I am having difficulties getting my watch repaired. Although I could live without it in George River it won't be the same in Sugluk, as with a bigger population I shall have to have organised clinics. Sugluk Eskimos apparently aren't quite so primitive, they are more used to the white man's ways.

August 30th 1969

The Nordair DC4 for Great Whale River on Wednesday (27th) was supposed to leave at 12.30 but was postponed first until 5, then 6 then 7. It finally left at 7.30. I wish I could have photographed the full moon shining amongst the clouds. It was quite spectacular flying through the silver clouds. A young British couple who are teachers, were on the same flight. This was their first experience of the Arctic and they bombarded me with questions. They will be working in Great Whale.

We landed in Great Whale River about midnight and I think the entire population (Great Whale has a population of approximately 600 Eskimos and 400 Cree Indians) was out to meet us, all milling around the plane. I knew that John Masty, a Cree Indian, the nursing station caretaker-cum-driver-Cree interpreter, would be there to meet me but I didn't attempt to find him as I knew he would find me. Suddenly a very flustered looking woman (Bunny Quarterman) came up to me and asked if I was the nurse. She welcomed me with open arms! Bunny is a teacher and Ora, who it seemed, was not here after all, had left Bunny in charge of the nursing station until either Ora returned from 'somewhere up the coast' or I arrived. Bunny had had a stressful time and was relieved to see a real nurse. An Indian woman had phoned one night to say she was having a heart attack. Bunny gave her some aspirin and told her to wait for the nurse. She later learned that this Indian, from another settlement, was looking for a bed for the night. Bunny picked John out of the crowd and they took me to the nursing station. Bunny had very kindly cooked me a chicken which was in the oven. She is so kind.

The nursing station is bigger than Chimo hospital! I feel quite lost in it. As Ora had been busy moving things around (one of her favourite occupations apparently) and had not finished before she was called away, it is almost impossible to find anything. The clinics have been non-stop as the population soon heard that there was a 'real' nurse here, after so long. I have had a lot of Indians coming to ask me for their bush medicines. I had no idea what they meant but Bunny explained that the Indians spend most of the winter living in tents in the bush, hunting, and are issued with a bag of medicines for each family. After routing around the nursing station, I came across a pile of bags and instruction booklets. The medicines are numbered 1,2,3 etc. and instructions (in Cree) tell them what each is for. The Indians are apparently being flown out to the bush on Monday (weather permitting) so I will be able to give the medicines out beforehand. I have the impression that the Indians are more demanding than the Eskimos. Apparently Eskimos and Indians don't mix at all. Bunny has tried all sorts of ways of mixing them in the classroom but as soon as it is time for recess, they go back to their own. She also told me that Great Whale, which is about two miles across, is divided into four residential quarters:

Eskimos, Cree Indians, federal government employees and provincial government employees.

Yesterday I saw and examined Rhoda, an Eskimo woman who looked suspiciously on the point of going into labour. It took me over an hour in the evening to find everything I would need for a delivery and prepare a room, 'just in case'. At 7 o'clock this morning I was not surprised to have a phone call (they have phones here) from Lucy, our Eskimo interpreter, to say that Rhoda was in labour. I asked Lucy to bring Rhoda to the nursing station if possible. She rang back later to say that they had started out for this mile walk across the sand but had to turn back. John was out hunting, our jeep was in a garage somewhere (I had no idea where) so I phoned the police to ask them to fetch Rhoda, which they kindly did. At 11 a.m. Rhoda delivered baby Isaac, a lovely baby 8lbs 8oz. As it is Saturday today there is no clinic so I just have Rhoda and Isaac to look after. Bunny keeps coming in to make me cups of coffee and wash my dishes etc. She is tremendous company and so thoughtful. She has spent several years in the Arctic.

September 10th 1969

Last Monday, September 1st, a plane came in from Port Harrison but much to everyone's surprise Ora wasn't on it. Someone brought me two patients en route to hospital, an Eskimo woman and a little girl of eight. I had no idea what the procedure for this was but John explained that he or Lucy would find homes for them until the next plane south. The woman had friends here, so she went to stay with them. Lucy went to find a home for the little girl. The poor child looked so lost, I sat her in with Rhoda and Isaac in the meantime; I knew Rhoda would chat to her. Lucy phoned shortly after to say that someone was on the way to fetch the child. When the woman arrived, the little girl was nowhere to be seen! Rhoda told me she had left a few minutes earlier without a word. We looked out of the window to see a small figure running towards the airstrip. What a predicament! The poor child was obviously terrified to stay here.

What was I going to do? I was responsible for whatever was going to happen. Lucy, who had just returned, immediately ran after her. At this moment who should walk in the door but Ora! I have never been so relieved to see anyone, after five days of trying to cope with a brand new environment. Lucy came back with the child in tow. She apparently told Lucy she had an aunt here and she had just gone to find her. This proved to be true so Lucy escorted her to the aunt's house. I breathed another sigh of relief. Ora's immediate need was a cup of tea and as it was suddenly miraculously quiet after these five hectic days, we sat down to become acquainted.

After hearing so much about Ora from Carolyne, Eileen, Mlle Laurin and John Masty, I already felt I knew her. It was very relaxing to chat with her and I knew we would get on very well and have fun. She has been working in the Arctic since the early '60s and has a lot of experience. Her job as zone nursing officer means she supervises all the nurses on the Hudson Bay coast and Sugluk. She is based in the Montreal office and visits us two or three times a year.

Ora explained what was going to happen: on Wednesday the 3rd, two brand new nurses, Ginette and Louisette, neither of whom had ever been in the Arctic, would be arriving and staying here in Great Whale. She said she would like me to continue running the clinic for a few days while she gave the new girls their orientation and then she and I will go to Sugluk together where she will give me mine. We also have to fit in a visit to Ivujivik before the freeze-up. After we had finished our tea Ora proceeded to show me some of the paperwork, which to me seems overwhelming. When patients go south to hospital, we have to write comprehensive case histories, fill out admission forms and get patients to sign consent forms, all this in quadruplicate! Ora also explained the planes and procedure to me. This is a much busier place than George River, with at least one plane every day. The DC4 comes in once a week from Montreal, Austin Airways' DC3 comes in three times a week from Timmins and Moosonee. Austin Airways continue up the coast, weather permitting and stop here again on the way back. All patients going south from Sugluk, Ivujivuk, Povungnituk and

Port Harrison stop here. It all seems rather complicated at the moment until I get a clearer idea of the geography of the Hudson Bay. John liaises with the airline office and organises tickets.

On Tuesday we had a very sick baby in the nursing station. Her parents were with her and while she was fairly stable Ora and I sat down to our well-earned steak supper, having not had time to eat all day. My plate was in front of me when there was a sudden cry from the father, the baby was convulsing. Ora found out that there was a Beech in so arranged for the pilot to fly the baby to Fort George hospital, an hour from here. (Fort George has mainly a Cree Indian population with a few Eskimo families). I had to abandon my beautiful meal to take the baby. She convulsed most of the way but there was nothing I could do. It was dark when we landed so there was no question of returning that night. We were actually lucky to have been able to land at all. After admitting the baby to the hospital it was 10 p.m. and I kept thinking of the steak supper which I had had to abandon. The hospital is run by nuns and I was shown to the nurses' home where I was given a room for the night. I asked if I could possibly have something to eat and was told that as it was someone's birthday, there was a party with refreshments in the sitting room. "Thank goodness!" I thought, "Lots of food!" However, the 'refreshments' consisted of minute two inch square sandwiches and I could have devoured them all. Naturally, I ate as many as possible within polite limits but this just added insult to injury and I could have wept every time I thought of that beautiful steak. I enjoyed talking to the nurses and the doctor though. Despite my hunger, I slept and was woken at 8 a.m. for breakfast. My first real meal in over 24 hours. We left at 9 o'clock and I was back here at 10 o'clock.

Louisette and Ginette arrived on the Wednesday, for their very first experience of the north. We all had a delicious uninterrupted meal of roast chicken that evening. They seem to be enjoying it so far. I have been holding the fort with the clinics while Ora has been showing Louisette and Ginette around etc. I seem to be spending all my spare time typing, as there are 16 patients going south on the next plane. We haven't had more than four or five hours sleep a night all week.

On Saturday Louisette and I had a trip out to the Belcher Islands in the Hudson Bay, about 20 minutes flight from here, to fetch a sick baby. Another regulation is that whenever we fly anywhere, even if it is only a 20 minute flight, we must take our Arctic sleeping bags and a box of four days' supply of food in case the weather should close in and we end up in the middle of nowhere or get stranded on an island. I hope (secretly) this will happen to me one day! The food box is always kept stocked up (with mainly dehydrated food) and the sleeping bags are nearby. Jim, the Bay manager on the Belcher Islands, is the lay dispenser as there is no nurse permanently stationed there, and he does a very good job. He is Scottish. The baby was a year old and had had a severe chest infection. He was very restless and we had to take turns holding him on the plane. I suspect he was over the worst by then.

On Monday (September 8th) Ora and I were supposed to leave for Sugluk but there was no plane. Yesterday's plane was going to Cape Dorset without stopping so we had to wait until this morning. We set off in the Canso, a very clumsy and heavy amphibian plane which can take off and land on land or in water. It is a Portuguese war plane apparently. You have to climb up a ladder and in through the door on the glass dome at the top. It was packed full of cargo and Ora and I were squeezed into a little corner. After 45 minutes fog closed in on us and we had to return to Great Whale! The others laughed when they saw us back again so soon! Tomorrow Ora and I plan to fly to Sugluk and pick up the X-ray machine before going on to Ivujivik. Time is running out if we need to spend a few days there and get back to Sugluk for my orientation, all before the freeze-up, as Ora has to be back in Montreal before then.

Sugluk: Peter & Moses with canoe which took us to Ivujivik

CHAPTER 4
IVUJIVIK

September 21st 1969

On September 11th we had another attempt to reach Sugluk. The weather there was good. We got as far as Port Harrison and hit a snow storm. The plane turned round and headed west. We had visions of ending up in Churchill on the west coast of the Hudson Bay. The pilot, who was new to the area, tried unsuccessfully to head round the storm but finally we had to land in Povungnituk (commonly known as POV). We went to the nursing station and Nora, the nurse looked after us. She is also English and has been there several years. She is actually leaving soon and two new nurses will be going to POV. As there are 600 Eskimos there they need two nurses. Ora and I managed to do a bit of shopping at the Hudson's Bay store and stock up with some food for Ivujivik. The next day was clear but as it had snowed a lot in the night it took the pilots hours to scrape all the snow off the wings before we could leave. The flight was about an hour and a half and we spent almost the entire time sorting out which boxes were to be left in Sugluk and which we were to take with us into Ivujivik. The co-pilot came to ask us to sit down as we were rocking the plane! Ora, who knows the coast like the proverbial back of the hand, pointed out various landmarks and I watched as we flew over the beautiful fjord-like entrance to Sugluk, my heart racing with increasing excitement and anticipation as Sugluk finally appeared! What a beautiful spot, surrounded by mountains and the sky was clear blue. I could hardly believe I had made it this far. The Canso dived into the water and for a moment it felt like being in a submarine. Canoes came out to fetch us and we got ready to unload all the Sugluk boxes.

Soon we learned that the weather was 'out' in Ivujivik and the pilot would not go in there with the Canso. It is very difficult landing in Ivujivik apparently, at the best of times. The entrance between the steep cliffs is very narrow and winds can be difficult there too. Not ideal for a heavy plane like the Canso. So we had to empty out all our stuff and take it to the nursing station. We tried to charter a Beech which was supposed to be in Wakeham Bay but it wasn't. We would have to wait another day. Ora took me to meet the Anglican missionary Chris Williams, whose wife Rona is a nurse and has been holding the fort these past months until I arrived. Chris and Rona, who are British, have been here six years and have a little boy, Andrew, who is four. Andrew speaks fluent Inuktituk as he has spent his whole life here. Apparently, Rona told us, when they go back to England on holiday and relatives ask Andrew how he likes living with the Eskimos, he doesn't understand. As far as he is concerned, he is one. We had a cup of tea with them and Ora took me round to meet some of the other white people. There are about 15 here. We then went to the nursing station, which was to be mine for the next 12 months. It was crammed full of boxes as all the annual supplies which arrived on the ship had not yet been unpacked. I was longing to get it all tidied up and arranged how I wanted it.

In the evening Father Verspeek, the Catholic missionary, was showing his weekly Friday evening film in the mission hall so we went to that and met more people. Ora tried to get Fort Chimo on the radio to charter a plane for tomorrow but the radio was 'out' too! It was now Friday and Ora had to be back here in Sugluk by Tuesday as Dr Savoie and Mlle Laurin were to visit Sugluk for a few days before they would all leave together for Montreal. A couple of Eskimos, Peter and Moses, had obviously heard about our plight and came to tell us that they were leaving for Ivujivik the following morning by canoe and offered to take us. Ora agreed and they told us to dress very warmly as it was a long journey (90 miles). Someone lent Ora a ski-doo suit and I had plenty of warm clothes. We then had to cut down on our luggage so only took our sleeping bags, enough food for the journey, the X-ray equipment and vaccines. Ora knew there was a good supply of dehydrated food at the health centre in Ivujivik so we wouldn't starve.

We left about 8 a.m. the next morning (Saturday September 13th). After passing through the fjord, we were soon out on the open sea, the Hudson Strait. It was raining and misty and the first snow had fallen on the mountains. Peter and Moses looked after us as we had never been looked after before! They made us a nice little place to sit in the bottom of the boat and covered us and our equipment with a sheet of plastic. They kept feeding us chocolate bars from time to time and asked frequently if we were OK. I found this most touching. It was quite rough at times and spray from the high waves came into the boat. By one o'clock we were all rather cold so they pulled into land, set up a tent and lit a stove. We ate our sandwiches and after a hot drink, we soon warmed up enough to continue our journey. It got colder and rougher all the time so by the time we arrived in Ivujivik we were somewhat damp and tired after this nine hour journey. All the Eskimos (population about 110) were out to greet us and Steve, the lay dispenser, invited us up to his house for supper. He had to lend Ora a pair of trousers as she was soaked! Poor Ora - she suffers from the cold. Later, when my fur had dried, it was full of lumps of salt! Steve is a lovely man, so welcoming and had cooked us a delicious meal of dehydrated stew and potatoes. It was good to sit down and relax in the warm.

There was no time to lose however; we had to start work as soon as we had eaten. We gathered everyone in the school and started the TB testing first as it takes 48-72 hours before the reactions to the tests can be read. We finished them all about midnight and after tidying up we were thankful to crawl into our sleeping bags for the night. The health centre is just a primitive little cabin with two rooms partitioned off the main room, very like George River but smaller.

Sunday was not a holiday for us but as all the Eskimos were in church between ten and twelve, we had time to set up the X-ray machine and dark tent in the school. We had to use the school as it is the only building with a powerful enough electricity supply for the X-ray machine. It is also the most spacious. Ora took the X-rays and I worked in the dark tent, developing them and changing cassettes. That was great fun. Ben the builder kindly invited us to supper so we had an hour's break. The Eskimos didn't seem to mind having to come out late in the evening at all. Unfortunately, the X-ray machine broke down and developing was taking longer and longer as we had not been able to bring enough developer and fixer solutions, so we had to stop. By now it was 3 a.m. anyway.

We had an early start on Monday morning to do the immunisations. Ora managed to fix the X-ray machine so we did a few more before the machine packed up again. We weren't sure if a plane was coming that day so we had to be ready to go at a moment's notice. We did some medicals in the afternoon and started reading the TB test results that evening.

On Tuesday we continued our work, still ready to leave if necessary, when suddenly we heard a plane overhead so rushed round frantically gathering all our things together. However, it circled round three times and took off again; the pilot obviously didn't like the look of the water. We had also been to see Peterjusi, an old man with pneumonia who was dying. We managed to fix up some oxygen for him and later Ora and I took it in turns to sit with him and the family. I was with him when he finally died at 7 p.m. His family had been sitting with him and it was all very peaceful. This was my first Eskimo death so I was rather sad. Peterjusi had apparently told his son he was going to die that day. Two women immediately started to wash him and get him ready for the funeral the next day. There was a church service that evening so we didn't make much progress with the immunisations as everyone was in church.

Peterjusi's funeral was the next morning so Ora and I went to that. Everyone seemed so appreciative for what we had done and that we went to the funeral. It was a very simple little service and the entire population was there. They had made a coffin out of plywood with a cross on the top. Afterwards they took the coffin on the muskeg (a tractor-like vehicle, the only vehicle in Ivujivik) up on the hill and buried him there. It was cold up there but everyone went up and afterwards everyone shook hands with everyone else. Funerals are usually the day after the death as the Eskimos don't like to keep bodies in the house. It can take hours with permafrost just to dig a shallow grave, even in the summer. In winter it can take several men a whole day. At 4 p.m. we heard that the plane had left Sugluk so at 5 o'clock we were ready on the beach. At 5.30 we heard that the plane had had to turn round and return to Sugluk! So we had another evening for immunisations until 11 p.m. By now it was Thursday and we should already have been in Sugluk. We were waiting on the beach from 8.30 the next morning and the little single engine Dornier finally landed on the water at 9.30. This was really it! The children had had quite a holiday from school all week. I was sad to leave Ivujivik; these Eskimos are so unspoiled and helpful. It reminded me very much of George River.

CHAPTER 5
SUGLUK

Ora and I left Ivujivik on Thursday September 18th with a single engine Dornier that Dr Savoie had chartered from Chimo for us. On our flight back I began to see how dangerous our trip along the Hudson Strait in a canoe could have been. The cliffs were sheer into the water almost all the way except for the spot where we put up the tent for our break.

We arrived in Sugluk about 10.30 a.m. I was longing to get settled down in Sugluk and have an uninterrupted year here, really get to know the people and look after them as well as teaching them how to look after themselves. During my time in Great Whale I gained a fair idea of what would be expected of me and I am ready to put in everything I have. First of course, Ora was going to give me my orientation which would expand on what I had learned and explain procedures specific to Sugluk.

The water sprayed around us as we landed on the bay in Sugluk and we were taken by canoe to the village. Dr Savoie and Pauline Laurin were waiting for us in the health centre, having arrived the previous day. I thought they seemed rather cool, perhaps angry that we hadn't been there to meet them when they arrived. They probably didn't know we were still stuck in Ivujivik. This was the first time I had met Dr Savoie, the director of medical services and it struck me she was not happy about our trip to Ivujivik. I mentioned this to Ora and she said it was just her manner and laughed it off. I wasn't entirely convinced though and suspected that Ora was in trouble and protecting me. (I learned later that she was). To our surprise they told us they were not staying as planned but leaving that afternoon. Not only that but they were taking Ora with them. This was a bit of a shock to me. Was I ready to be on my own?

They left about 3 o'clock. The plane took off from the bay and slowly disappeared from sight behind the mountains. Only the throb of the engine could still be heard for a few moments. I turned back towards the health centre feeling slightly abandoned, now solely responsible for these people and 1500 miles from headquarters in Montreal. I was sad to lose Ora so suddenly like that - and I didn't get my orientation. As I let myself into my health centre all feeling of desolation left me to be quickly replaced by a sense of excitement. After all this was what I had wanted all along, a year in a small post. It has taken seven months to get here! Everywhere was piled high with boxes, crates, parcels and mail which would have to be unpacked and put away, a job after my own heart! I shall be able to organise everything how I want. I could hardly wait to get started. The desk was also piled high with correspondence for the Administrator, Lab technician, Pharmacist, Radiology dept., Central Supplies dept. And Operating Room! All destined for the wastepaper basket. The nursing stations and health centres are apparently registered as hospitals so we receive the same kind of promotional material as hospitals. To my joy, I also found two letters from home waiting for me.

Several patients came to see me that evening. Most, I suspect to see what I was like and I had to be firm and tell them to come back at 9 o'clock the next day, for the clinic. One little boy however did need urgent attention, he had a fractured collar bone. It took me a long time to find the bandages amongst all the clutter. Poor little chap, he was so miserable. Fortunately bandaging relieves the pain.

My residence is a 50 foot trailer just behind the health centre. It has two bedrooms, a bathroom with hot and luke-warm running water (as there is an element in the water tank to stop the water freezing there is no cold water). In Sugluk we have the 'honey bag' system for the toilet: a black bag is placed in the toilet bowl with some Elsan fluid and every week I have to take the bag out carefully, tie a knot in the top and put it outside where it is collected on a truck, taken out and thrown into the sea. The clean water supply is in a covered tank with a Formica work top in the kitchen. We get water delivered once a week. There is a drainage tank under the trailer which also gets emptied from time to time. The oil-fired central heating has two furnaces so that if one breaks down the other automatically takes over. There is a record player in my sitting area. I never envisaged such luxury. I would have been happier to live in the primitive health centre and have the clinic in the trailer. I did say that to Ora the other day and she laughed. There are two electricity generators in the village which are used alternately. The white people have internal telephones, the 15 of us share the same line and we each have our own ring. My ring is two shorts and one long, one turn for a short and four turns for a long. A general ring for everyone is eight turns. For example if there is information about a plane or to say that the mail is ready to be picked up then everyone answers. At the moment I find it hard not to pick the phone up every time it rings! I suppose I'll get used to it. I have heard clicks on the line when a call has been for me. I suspect people are curious to know who wants the nurse. So nothing can be private here either!

I also have my own little red ski-doo called a 'Sno-Ro'. It is sitting outside the trailer at the moment. We have had some snow so it won't be long before I can use it. The village is much bigger than I had anticipated and my place is at one end of it so I shall need my Sno-Ro in the winter. Mary is my interpreter, a sweet Eskimo girl, about 19 I think. She also does the cleaning.

I am already busy typing records for six patients who need to go to hospital, two of whom we brought back with us from Ivujivik. The freeze-up will be wonderful with only the daily records to keep up to date and no mail at all coming in.

I have ordered four months' supply of food from Timmins! The biggest order I have ever done in my life. There is a big supermarket (Blahey's) near the airport in Timmins and we give the Austin Airways pilot our shopping lists. He passes them to Mr. Blahey who makes sure our orders are on the next flight and the bill goes to Montreal. I have ordered 16 dozen eggs amongst other things.

Sugluk health centre

October 14th 1969

I have been here for three weeks now and haven't had time to sit down and write. Initially I was rather disappointed with Sugluk, my heart was still in George River and I suspect will be for some time. But I am going to enjoy it here in a different way. From the work point of view there is much more scope and of course it is better organised. One thing which did upset me was the fact that whites and Eskimos don't mix socially but at least as the nurse I shall have a lot of contact with Eskimos through work.

I am getting used to my luxury trailer and have made all sorts of discoveries: an electric sewing machine which, needless to say, won't be used by me, and an extraordinary collection of dehydrated foods: potato, stews, eggs and whipped cream topping, the latter in massive quantities. My predecessor must have been addicted to it. I can regulate the central heating myself. I wouldn't say this was wasted on me but I am the very one who would be happy living in a primitive cabin. I do however appreciate the unlimited hot water. I have to boil water for drinking and keep it in the fridge or drink Seven-Up, (like fizzy lemonade) which Ora insisted I buy by the case from the Bay.

My first week was spent unpacking all the annual supplies in the health centre and arranging everything how I wanted it until there wasn't a spare corner anywhere. It was such a satisfying job and I worked late into the night to get it finished. I must have thrown out over 100 empty cartons. Now the floor has been polished, (not by me) I am thrilled with my health centre and am now ready to be able to start baby clinics. All the under-fives have to be seen once a month so I am going to start with the 1969 babies. I think the easiest thing is to have clinics for each year separately as the Eskimos seem to be able to remember dates of birth better than actual ages. My sick clinic hours are from 9 a.m. till 12 p.m. and afternoons are for TB clinics, baby clinics, home visits and school visits. And of course, paper work!

Steve, in Ivujivik is very devoted and reliable. He calls on the radio whenever he has a problem and I can prescribe over the radio or suggest what he could do.

I was anticipating lots of time for cooking here, to take advantage of my super-modern kitchen and unlimited food. Last Saturday I had my first attempt at baking bread and had just reached the kneading stage when I was interrupted for a sick baby. When I returned to my bread an hour later, it had started rising and I was wondering what to do about it when I was called out again for the same baby, so I put the dough, as it was, in the oven and baked it quickly before taking the baby in for the night. By now she was convulsing. I was up all night with her and managed to catch up with some paper work during the night. By the morning the baby was a bit better so I sent her home and went home to get a few hours sleep. The bread meanwhile was surprisingly edible, though rather stodgy. I was kept pretty busy with the baby as she was obviously very ill so arranged for her to be evacuated on Tuesday on the last plane out. Ora, who was still down the coast, came up to escort her. It was good to see her and we managed to have a chat on the plane before it took off again. So the freeze-up has begun! My eggs arrived safely and I have stored them in the second porch area where the fridge-freezer is. (There is no heating in that porch).

The temperatures have been in the 30s and we have a sprinkling of snow but the real winter hasn't begun yet. We have had some strong winds but I gather nothing to the gales we shall be getting later on. My trailer was apparently moved from the

Hudson's Bay property last year and as there was no more room in the centre of the village it was moved here, which is more exposed. I don't know how it will stand up to the gales.

The Maclean ship is here at the moment with various annual supplies for the village. It is anchored four or five miles around the corner and they have their own helicopter which makes several trips a day here, so it's quite a common sight. The ship will stay about a week before moving on to the next place. Later it works as an ice-breaker up the St. Lawrence River. On Sunday, some of us were invited to dinner on the ship. Father Verspeek was to give Mass before the dinner. The helicopter came to fetch us in pairs starting about 11 o'clock, which was 10 o'clock their time so by the time we had had Mass and sat drinking punch for an hour it was 2 p.m. our time before we sat down to dinner. What a terrific dinner! With so many courses it took an over an hour. I didn't need to eat anything else that day. We were then given a tour of the ship and shown the radio equipment, radar and weather forecast charts, not that any of us understood much though, except Father Verspeek who is very mechanically minded. About 5 p.m. the helicopter ferried us all home again. As we were taken from land to ship we didn't even get our feet wet. On the way back the pilot did a few flips and turns for excitement and told us, "When we get over the village, I'll show you what it's like when the engine cuts out." He was as good as his word! I would hate to experience that in reality.

Father Verspeek brought me a bag of mussels the other day. They are collected at low tide and are delicious when fresh. There is no fishing here at the moment but the fish will return once the ice starts forming.

Yesterday was Harvest Thanksgiving and there was an English service. English services are held every two weeks. It seemed strange to be singing Harvest hymns with snow outside and not an apple in sight. I have actually been able to take the weekend off for a change, having only had one day off since I started in Great Whale.

Now I am beginning to get to know the other white people and feel part of the community. Father Verspeek is Dutch and has been up here for 20 years. When he first arrived in Sugluk, it was by ship - there were no planes in those days. As the ship sailed away he knew he would not see another white man for a year, apart from a Hudson's Bay trader perhaps. Just one ship a year to bring in all the provisions and a year's supply of coal for the village. Eskimos were still living in igloos at that time and Father Verspeek told me that if the igloo was well built it would last about three months. He built his house and as I mentioned, is very mechanically minded. He can fix ski-doos, watches, furnaces and he has also had a lot of dental experience (like most missionaries, I gather). As I am strictly speaking, responsible for doing dental extractions we have an arrangement with Montreal that if we are happy for the missionaries to continue, all we need do is sign an agreement. I have already handed over all the dental equipment to him! A patient with toothache has to come to me first then I sign a referral to Father Verspeek. Actually, some years ago he went on a short course with a dentist and as well as learning where to inject, he learned a bit about fillings. Naturally, if anyone needs antibiotics I give them out. I am only too delighted to let him be the dentist and he is happy to continue. On a Friday evening all the whites gather at the mission hall and he shows us films that are sent up at regular intervals. It's quite a social occasion, followed by coffee and chat.

Chris (the Anglican missionary) and Rona run Girl Guides, Boy Scouts and women's meetings amongst other things. Rona also relieves the nurse for holidays. A very nice couple and Andrew is a cute little red head. I believe there are the occasional red-headed or blue-eyed Eskimos dotted around the Arctic, thanks to some of the early traders, I understand. None in Sugluk as far as I know.

Lorenzo (French Canadian) is the administrator for the provincial government and radio telephone operator. His wife Madonne teaches kindergarten. They have a little girl of five and two-year-old twins. They have been here for about five years.

Don (English Canadian) is the administrator for the federal government. He seems very shy and tends to keep very much to himself. This is his second year here but I understand he spent several years in Frobisher Bay (Baffin Island).

Lucien (French Canadian), the mechanic and his wife Laurette have been here several years. They have three children who all go to the federal school with the Eskimos.

Joan and Nelson are a young English Canadian couple who have just started their second year here. They are both teachers in the federal school.

Michael and Elizabeth (English Canadian) arrived a couple of weeks before I did. Michael is a teacher (federal) and Elizabeth, who incidentally is also a nurse, has her hands full with a 17-month-old boy and a 7 month baby girl.

Terry is the Bay manager and is new to Sugluk but not to the Arctic. I haven't yet met his wife Vera as she is at home in Ireland, having a baby. They are both Irish. Terry is good fun.

Michelle and Ruth (French Canadian) are both teachers in the provincial school and have five pupils between them! These five and the kindergarten children are the only ones at that school. Most of the Sugluk children go to the federal school.

So I think we are a lovely bunch of people and I feel we are all good friends despite the potential for political conflict between the two governments.

My name has accumulated quite a lot of variations from Nincrop to Musgrove! Lorenzo is the only one who knows how it is spelled as he often has to spell it out over the radio: Mike, Oscar, Sierra, Sierra, Charlie, Romeo, Oscar, Papa.

October 18th 1969

A beautiful sunny day, temperatures in the 20s. We have had a couple of snow storms already and there is a two foot snow drift outside my trailer. The trailer faces south which happens to be where the most severe storms come from. I have tried my Sno-Ro but there is still not quite enough snow for it yet. I find it quite difficult to start. It starts by pulling a cable after switching on the ignition.

On Thursday evening Lucien caught a white whale. In no time the Eskimos had it laid out on the snow, degutted and cut into small pieces for everyone in the village. They are so quick cutting with their semi-circular knives. Even children soon learn to use these knives without harming themselves. Eskimos eat mainly with their hands but will use these blades to cut raw meat. They usually eat meat and fish raw.

October 29th 1969

Some Eskimos were going to Deception Bay today so I gave them a letter home for them to post from there as they have plane contact all year round.

We have had quite a bit more snow in the past couple of weeks and temperatures are now going below the 20s.

Last weekend I took my Sno-Ro out properly for the first time. As well as finding it difficult to start, I'm also having trouble steering it but I'm determined to master it. Every Sunday afternoon the white people go for a ski-doo outing, led by Father Verspeek or Lucien, so I set off with them. It was a beautiful day and Father Verspeek led us across the mountains. We were heading for a lake about 15 miles away. After struggling for a couple of miles to stay on the track, I discovered one of my skis was hanging off! Father Verspeek had a look at it and said it would be best to leave it there so I sat on the back of Terry's komautik with Michaël. We hadn't been going very long before Terry found that his track was slipping. We had long ago been left behind and it was about an hour before he got it going again. As it was below zero it was pretty cold not moving but we were all dressed for the weather. A little later, we came across Michelle's skidoo abandoned with a hole in the petrol tank. By the time we reached the lake the others were just turning round to go home. They imagined we had already gone back. There was still a little coffee left and we drank it thankfully. It was getting dark by this time so we had to take it slowly. Nelson and Joan managed to hit a rock and bend a ski but they were OK. We were all rather exhausted after this long trip, 35 miles in five hours. A Sunday afternoon adventure!

This Sunday the clocks went back and there has been confusion ever since as we weren't sure if we were going to change ours. It seems a pity to take away another hour of daylight. Eventually, we had to because of radio telephone hours. So now, it gets dark at 4.30 p.m. Steve in Ivujivik is not changing his clocks but will respect our radio hours. A pity we have to conform with civilisation. If we have been confused, it will take the Eskimos even longer I suspect. George River doesn't have this problem!

I eventually managed to see all the babies in clinics (my system of clinics by year of birth is working well. Now, I have to start all over again with the 1969 babies. On Friday afternoons Mary cleans the health centre so I do my school visiting then.

Father Verspeek has fixed my ski-doo and this afternoon he and I went for a little trip into the mountains. I am getting the hang of it now and it feels much easier. Father Verspeek was surprised I got as far with it as I did last weekend. What beautiful scenery it is round here, even though there are no trees. We had a magnificent view over the bay.

Chris has started giving lessons in Inuktituk so I went along. Amongst other things, I learned that nouns have seven cases (like Latin - actually I can't remember how many there were in Latin but there were quite a few) and there are no articles.

November 7th 1969

Last Friday was Hallowe'en and Canadians go in for it in a big way so there were lots of parties. The schoolchildren had spent the week making masks and they all went to school in fancy dress. There were plenty of games and Joan had made toffee apples for her class, a rare treat for Eskimos. In the evening the children did the rounds of the houses and collected sweets etc. We had a fancy dress party and I went as a witch. Everyone had brought food and we had more than enough to eat.

We have had some strong gales and my two foot snow drift doubled, burying my ski-doo. I managed to dig it out but because it was all packed with hard snow I had to ask Father Verspeek to start it up again for me. I have taken advantage of afternoon trips with either Father Verspeek or Chris, on days when I don't have any clinics or visits. Then I do my office work later in the evening. I suppose as the days shorten the afternoons will barely exist. I would rather take advantage of daylight while we still have it. We had a sudden thaw a few days ago because temperatures went up into the 30s then during the night it froze and my front door was iced over so I couldn't open it. I phoned Don and asked if he could send someone over to let me out. An Eskimo came straightaway and apparently reported back to Don, "Nurse not strong"! Now because of the ice, everyone is having trouble with ski-doos. Mine got stuck on full throttle one day and I was heading for the village, totally out of control. What a nightmare! I was terrified! I threw myself off it and lay in the snow watching as it hared off towards a lamp post. Sure enough, it hit the lamp post and I saw snow shaken off the lamp post with the impact. I approached cautiously, expecting the worst but the engine was still running and the ski-doo had come to a neat halt, one ski either side of the post! I managed to turn off the throttle but was too scared to use it again until Father Verspeek (what would I do without him?) had fixed it, which he did and it is now fine again.

November 17th 1969

We have certainly had some strange weather lately. Last weekend we had a terrific storm with gale force winds, lasting 36 hours. It was almost impossible to stand up and the noise was fantastic. I think I was the only one to brave it outside but I had several patients to visit. All the loose snow was blown away leaving just ice underfoot. I was bowled over once and just rolled until I hit something to stop me. I was praying that all the old people would stay in. We then had a four day thaw and now it is freezing again, there is treacherous ice everywhere. Temperature now down to 18 again.

Terry and Lorenzo are dead set on getting a plane in on the lake, up in the mountains so we decided to go up there again on Saturday for our weekend outing to see what it was like. There was hardly any snow left after the storm so it was hard going until we got up higher. At one stage we had to come off the usual track and go down a very steep hill, the top few feet were almost vertical. I was last in line but when I reached that first slope, I panicked, didn't like the look of this one bit, and turned my ski-doo, the worst possible thing to do! The ski-doo skidded, I fell off and rolled down the hill with the ski-doo beside me. I tried unsuccessfully to get out of the way as I was terrified it was going to run over me. I eventually came to rest on some rocks about 20 feet down and the ski-doo also stopped right beside me, neither of us the worse for wear. It was apparently much worse for the onlookers, horrified, watching me come hurtling down the hill. Poor Terry was quite shaken. Father Verspeek could see I was trying to get away from the ski-doo and as I was apparently between the skis he was praying that I wouldn't succeed as I was actually preventing the skidoo from going any faster. The rest of the trip was uneventful and we found 20 inches of ice on the lake which is apparently enough for a plane to land. I would just as soon wait another few weeks and see the plane land on the bay. We started home about 3 o'clock and it was already getting dark. I was dreading going up Anne's Hill (as it has subsequently been christened) and it didn't help when I saw, ahead of me, Father Verspeek's ski-doo leap into the air those top couple of feet. However, I pointed my ski-doo straight up with full throttle, holding my breath. This time it was Madonne's and Ruth's downfall. Madonne had several attempts before she fell off and slipped a little way but her ski-doo went all the way to the bottom. Ruth was thrown off hers and hit her head on a rock, almost knocking herself out. Her ski-doo was OK. A couple of miles from the village, I had to abandon my ski-doo with carburettor problems. Another mile, Ruth had to abandon hers with a hole in the tank and Madonne's remained at the bottom of Anne's Hill. Those who stay home on these occasions are on tenterhooks until everyone is back again! All the ski-doos have now been collected and await their turn for repair. I'm not going up there again unless there is more snow.

November 20th 1969

I have now finished the baby clinics for this month and most of the babies have put on weight. They are all so different. The 1969 babies are gurgly and smiley and their tears short-lived. The 1968 babies are toddling around and looking at everything. Their tears are also short-lived. The 1967 children scream all the time, whether or not I do anything to them. Some of the 1966 ones are reasonable and others fight and kick. One bit me! The 1965 ones are very reasonable and brave about immunisations. Only one child ran away when his mother told him they were going to see the nurse. He was later found hiding in the co-op!

Today, I received a telegram from Moose Factory Hospital to say that the baby I evacuated in September has died. I had to get Chris to come with me to break the news to the family. I found this very upsetting naturally.

December 1st 1969

Saturday 22nd November was my 30th birthday! I am now starting a new decade. I don't feel old yet. I had a late breakfast and laid out all my birthday mail which I had received before the freeze-up. I received a collection of 'odds and ends' from the girls at Great Whale: chocolate, nuts, a Christmas pudding, some candles and a little stone carving of a seal. I already had my parents' present which was another rug-making kit but have not had much time for it yet. I did make one rug while I was in Chimo and George River and it took me three months. This one is obviously going to take longer. The afternoon was spent X-raying Ruth's hand as she hurt it falling over in last Thursday's storm. It took me over an hour to set up the X-ray machine and the dark tent, mix up the solutions and develop the X-ray. All for just one X-ray. As suspected, there was a fracture. I had previously bandaged her hand so there wasn't much else we could do. There was a party in the evening at Ruth and Michelle's place. It turned out to be a joint birthday party as Terry and

Joan's birthdays were on the 20th so we all shared a cake. It was a lovely party, good fun.

On Sunday we went up to the lake again and the men took oil barrels to outline the runway. The ice is now 21 inches thick, so quite adequate for a plane. Men have been up several times to prepare the strip. I enjoyed this trip more than any of the others partly because there is more snow and I am much more at ease with my ski-doo. I still ended up having to be brought home as one of my skis was damaged on some rocks near Anne's Hill.

Having spent all that time on Ruth's X-ray, it seemed such a waste to throw all the solutions away and I couldn't keep the dark tent up indefinitely. I decided to turn the health centre toilet into a dark room. I sealed over the window then passed the cable of the infra-red light through the ventilation slats before sealing them off. Then there were just a couple of cracks in other places to deal with. All the solutions go nicely along one wall and I sit on the toilet seat to work. If I do some of the chest X-rays every day, I shall be able to finish the whole village by January when Ora will be back again. The next thing was to try some chest X-rays as I wasn't sure where to begin. The instruction charts don't match this machine so Mary kindly offered to let me experiment with her. So, the pair of us, clad in lead aprons, after several attempts, eventually got the perfect picture. So I made notes on all this and actually called a couple of families this afternoon to do their X-rays. Having done 20 I waited till later to develop them. I had decided that if too many needed repeating I would wait until Ora came. I was delighted to find that only three needed repeating so I will carry on.

We had another violent 36 hour storm last week and my front door was blown off and smashed. It is now a write-off. School was cancelled and everyone stayed home. Father Verspeek reckoned that the wind was about 70 m.p.h. The next day, my inner porch door was iced up with all the snow and ice that had blown in so I had to climb out of the water delivery hatch which is about 18 inches square. The windows of course have metal mosquito netting over them so I can't get through them. I managed to push the door open from outside so now I know I shan't be stranded again.

On Thursday all the men went up to the lake and about 12.30 we heard a plane fly over. It was about 10 below here and would be even colder on the lake. I had mixed feelings about a plane so soon because I wanted to get all my files up to date, as well as doing more X-rays. On the other hand, the thought of having letters from home was very exciting. At 3 p.m. I heard the first ski-doos coming back and rushed to get through as many files as possible. The post would not be sorted before 4 and as my phone wasn't working I wouldn't hear Terry's general ring. I kept thinking about all the post I would have and was so excited that when my ski-doo wouldn't start, I just left it and hurried over to the Bay where to my great disappointment, learned that not only was there no post, the plane hadn't been able to land because of poor visibility. In the meantime all the outgoing mail is sitting in bags on the lake waiting for the plane which may try again on Wednesday. Our mail is apparently sitting in POV.

On Sunday we went for a ski-doo trip on the bay. Quite honestly I was frightened to think of all that water underneath the ice. The others attempted to reassure me that there was 14 inches of ice, almost enough for a plane to land on. I don't know if my fear is unfounded or not. Anyway, I went. It wasn't too cold and the snow on the ice was slushy and kept jamming up our ski-doo tracks between the skis. We didn't get very far as there always seemed to be someone in trouble. Suddenly we saw a seal pop its head out of a hole in the ice! Lucien and Lorenzo rushed for their guns while we watched it. We looked around for another hole but didn't see one. The seal popped its head out a few more times then disappeared. We thought it was probably trapped, not able to get out to sea. We saw some seal tracks where it must have come out looking for another hole. Seals can't go very far without coming up for air so it will have to wait for the break-up. For once, I got home on my own this time. It is now dark at 3 p.m. and it gets light about 9 a.m.

Sugluk: DC3 landing on a lake

December 13th 1969

I have now done over 200 X-rays so there are only about 90 still to do. It is very exciting and rewarding. I still get a thrill out of a good picture. I have been developing until 9 o'clock most evenings. I'm leaving the youngest babies until Ora comes in January.

We actually had our first plane last week. What excitement! After all the work we (or, at least the men) had, preparing the strip, the pilot wasn't happy with it or the wind was in the wrong direction or something so he circled round until he found a better spot, which happened to be another lake about seven miles from there. I didn't have time to go up anyway. The post was ready about 7 p.m. and the whole population seemed to be in the Bay. I had a sack full of rubbish for the lab technician, records dept. etc. I would have welcomed something for the X-ray technician this time but there was nothing for the X-ray Dept. I had lots of letters from home and friends which took me a few days to get through. Amongst others, a letter from Louise (my Fort Chimo friend) saying that the four nurses who were in Chimo have all left and Louisette has gone back to help. It's just as well I didn't stay in George River, I would definitely be back in Chimo again by now.

We are expecting another plane tomorrow. This one is going to land on an old runway about 13 miles away, on the other side of the bay. Now that the bay is completely frozen over, ski-doos can get over there to meet it. I have three patients to send out on it but they will be able to travel in the snowmobile. The snowmobile is like a small bus which runs on a track with skis at the front in winter and wheels in summer. The weather has been really good lately, temperatures usually about five or ten below zero - it even went down to 18 below one day. I have a way of knowing how to tell if it is below zero: I do what I call a 'sniff test': if my nostrils stick together as I sniff, it is zero or below. We are approaching the shortest day now. At the moment it gets light about 9.30 a.m. and dark about 2.30 p.m.

As a Christmas present to my parents this year I have decided to invite them to come and visit me in Sugluk in April. I really would like them to experience this while I'm still here and April is probably the best month. They can decide whether to come by ship or plane, or come one way and return another. I don't want them to be shocked by the amount of the cheque so I have told them it is only a few month's salary for me and I don't have anything much to spend it on here. Once they get to Montreal, Claire (whom they know), will look after them and get them on the flights up here.

December 31st 1969

I have had a non-stop month this month. I finished all the X-rays on the 17th, Elisabee turned up in labour in the early hours on the 18th and delivered a lovely eight pound baby boy. As she was fine, I let her go home that evening. Her brother came to fetch her on his ski-doo. I don't know what my midwifery tutors would think about that! The next day, Nunivak came and delivered a ten pound baby boy. She wanted to go home straightaway but I persuaded her to stay overnight as she didn't deliver until the afternoon. She went home by ski-doo the next morning. Unlike my deliveries in George River, I have proper delivery packs here with all the equipment, including cord clamps so I may never have to use fishing line again!

Rona told me a story of a British midwife she met several years ago who went to an Eskimo village in the days before nurses were sent to the Arctic and she asked the Eskimo midwife if she could observe a delivery. She promised just to observe, not to interfere. The day came and the English midwife stood back and observed. The woman in labour was lying on her caribou skin on her back with her knees up. A long skirt covered her knees. Several Eskimo women sat around for support. Suddenly the sound of a newborn's cry came from under the skirt but no-one made a move to intervene for quite a few minutes. Then, the Eskimo midwife lifted up the skirt, brought out the baby and dealt with the cord and the placenta. The English midwife was quite shocked and later asked the missionary why the baby was left for so long before being cared for. The missionary explained that they had to be sure that the baby was strong enough to survive on its own. Survival of the fittest.

After that hectic week with new mothers and babies and writing records for three patients going to hospital, I was really looking forward to my four days off over Christmas. There were lots of parties planned. Austin Airways had brought in some Christmas trees so I put one up in my trailer. When did I last see a tree?! Terry's wife, Vera also came back with her seven-week-old baby. Terry was over the moon to see her again. It must be hard to have to go out during break-up or freeze-up to have a baby.

At the end of term the schoolchildren put on a fantastic Christmas show. They sang songs in English, did a sketch in Eskimo, held a gym display and finally a Christmas pageant. What organisation that was! It was wonderful to see such enthusiasm. The schoolchildren are given two Christmas dinners with all the trimmings, one from the Anglican mission and the other from the Catholic mission.

We have now had about three planes so the mail is catching up but there is still a lot to come. Mr Blahey was on the last plane and took a lot of food orders for his supermarket. It must be interesting for him to put faces to names. He obviously takes great pride in getting our orders to us promptly on the next plane. That plane landed on the lake seven miles away, so I went in the snowmobile. Ruth, Michelle and Don went south for the Christmas holidays.

On the 22nd the Eskimos had a dance in the school. Several of them play instruments, violins and accordion. They like reels and square dances and each dance lasts about quarter of an hour. It was a very lively evening.

We had a combined Eskimo and English service on the 23rd and I read one of the lessons. The lessons were read first in Eskimo and then in English. The church was packed out. After the service there was a party at Chris and Rona's house.

On Christmas Eve Father Verspeek held Midnight Mass in French, English and Eskimo. (All the French Canadians here are Catholic). Afterwards we (the white people who were still here) had our Christmas dinner there, he certainly did us proud. It must have been 3 a.m. by the time I went home. My wonderful four day holiday had just begun!

At 12 p.m. I was woken for a very sick eight-month-old baby with pneumonia, who was struggling to breathe. I got up quickly and set up the oxygen tent and injected antibiotics. I nursed the baby all day, there was nothing more I could do. She was fairly stable in the evening so I got the mother to sit with the baby and I looked in on Madonne's party for a short while but couldn't really relax. I hadn't seen a soul all day and felt a little sorry for myself that I was so alone on Christmas day while everyone else was enjoying themselves. Lucien had been over with some ice for the oxygen tent but apart from him I had been alone with the baby. I found a tin of tuna in a cupboard in the health centre so that was my dinner on Christmas day. I sat with the baby all night, at least till 3.30 a.m. when she suddenly died. It was awful to watch the poor little thing fighting for her life, she must have been exhausted. If I had managed to save her, Christmas would not have been so sad but it was quite the saddest Christmas Day I have ever had. I then had to go and wake Chris and we went to break the news to the family. The Eskimos are very philosophical about death, they knew I had done my best and it was meant to be. Chris and I spent half an hour with the family and there was discussion about what to do with the body. The grandmother didn't want it in the house. I said I was quite happy for it to stay in the health centre so everyone set to work. Three men came over to make the coffin and a woman came with her sewing machine to make the shroud, while I cleared up. It was a hive of activity at 5 a.m. The mother sat there and people came in and out to sit with her. The baby was dressed in the shroud, which was a long white gown, with long sleeves and frilly cuffs. She also had a white bonnet with a frill. Just before the baby was put in the coffin, her face was covered so that only her hands, joined, were showing. When the coffin was ready, the baby was placed in it and everyone there came to shake the baby's hand, including myself, and the coffin was then nailed shut. It was taken to the church, ready for the funeral at 12 p.m. By now it was 7.30 and I went home to sleep until 11 o'clock. The funeral service lasted about 20 minutes in the church, followed by more prayers and hymns up on the hill. It was pretty cold up there, below zero. Once the coffin was covered over, there was more handshaking, everyone with everyone else. The family were very appreciative of all I had done (I didn't feel I had done much) and were only sorry that I had been on my own when the baby died.

I had several sick visits to do so those first two days of my holiday just disappeared. Joan and Nelson had their party on Sunday the 27th and I was able to enjoy that. On the Tuesday, I had only been in bed one hour when I was called for Evie who was pregnant, having an antepartum haemorrhage. She still had another five weeks to go. I sedated her and got Mary to sit with her while I went to Lorenzo's house to radio Frobisher Bay who are supposed to be on 24 hour duty. I had to wake Lorenzo up and he seemed a bit reluctant to get out of bed straightaway until Madonne had to explain to me that he was naked. I was very slow on the uptake. How embarrassing! Frobisher Bay failed to answer so I then had to go and wake Terry so he could try Coral Harbour on his radio. No luck there either. I knew there was a plane in POV so I asked Terry if he could contact them early in the morning and ask for a nurse to come and take Evie out. I went back to the health centre and sat up with Evie all night. By morning she was in a good deal of pain. I was unable to examine her because of the possibility of placenta praevia, (if the placenta was situated below the baby, examination could rupture the placenta, resulting in the baby's death). This was a midwife's nightmare. At 8.30 Lucien came to fetch us with the snowmobile and I took a delivery pack with me just in case. The plane was landing on the furthest lake, 15 miles away as the pilot couldn't yet land on the bay. It took us over an hour to get there and poor Evie had a very rough trip. We arrived about ten minutes before the plane but in the meantime, it was obvious Evie was in labour and she gave birth to a baby girl in the snowmobile. I hadn't thought to take anything to wrap a baby in but we wrapped her in a ski-doo suit and covered her with an atigi. By the time Lise, one of the new nurses from POV got out of the plane, both mother and baby were fine, placenta delivered and Evie had stopped bleeding. There was now no reason to send her out, so we bumped our way back to the health centre and Lise returned to POV. I weighed the baby and she weighed five pounds six ounces. Evie went home yesterday but I decided to keep the baby overnight just to make sure. Rona kindly came in to relieve me for a couple of hours during the evening. At 12 o'clock today I took the baby home. This evening, Thursday (New Year's Eve) Laurette and Lucien had their party which I was really able to enjoy. I can't believe it is 1970 already! And so to BED.

January 10th 1970 Sunday

This year has not started very well. I fell thankfully into my own bed at last after the New Year's Eve party. It was such a relief. It was not to be however; I was called 20 minutes later for Kinasasi who was having a miscarriage. The worst was over by the time I got there but I gave her an injection and sat with her awhile and once satisfied she was OK. I went home and back to bed. Five minutes later I was called for another baby with pneumonia! I took the baby in, set up the oxygen tent but he died at 3 a.m. The second death in just a few days! This time the family took the baby home to prepare him for the funeral. I had four hours sleep before having to get up for the morning clinic. Not a soul appeared before 11 o'clock and at 11.30 the health centre was packed out. The Eskimos find it hard to get out of bed in midwinter and have been coming later and later to clinic. I can't cope with trying to see everyone in half an hour! I had sick people to visit in the afternoon so it was all running very late. I decided it was high time I did something about it so I called everyone to a meeting in the school at 6 p.m. I explained to them that I was there to help them but they also had to help me. Clinic started at 9 o'clock, I told them and even if I had been up all night, I would be there at 9 o'clock. I could not see everyone before 12 o'clock if they didn't turn up till 11.30. I also had work to do in the afternoon. There were murmurings of agreement and understanding so I went home, hopefully to sleep this time. It was now Friday and I had hardly had any sleep since Monday night. They must have got the message because no-one came near me all weekend!

Saturday was my party but I hadn't been able to plan it with all the events of the week. I felt so much better after a good night's sleep and spent all day preparing for my party. Having never catered for more than four people, I was now preparing for 15. I made some bread rolls, hors d'oevres, home-made chicken soup and Arctic char pie (I had some char in the freezer), tinned Christmas pudding and fruit jelly. I didn't have any alcohol but one or two people brought bottles. My guests arrived about 9 p.m. We tend to start parties late so that people can put their children to bed first. It was great fun and I think everyone enjoyed themselves. I was quite proud of myself catering for such a big group! I was a bit concerned because Nelson and Father Verspeek have huge appetites. Nelson had four helpings of soup and three helpings of pie but no-one went home hungry as far as I know. Terry had brought some 'swinging' records and we danced so it was really good fun. Everyone had gone by 2 a.m. so I just hoovered up the nutshells (as I didn't have a nutcracker we were cracking nuts with a hammer on the floor), left the washing-up till the morning and went to bed. Another full night's sleep. This week has been back to normal (no funerals) and people have been coming to clinic earlier. I hope I never have to go through a time like that again. I can't help wondering if there was more I could have done to save those babies. I have now finished all the X-rays. There are a dozen Sugluk students who go to a training school in Great Whale who are home for the holiday and I have found them all for their X-rays as they wouldn't be included in the Great Whale population.

We had our first plane on the bay a couple of days ago, on the 8th. The ice on the bay is now 27 inches thick. If we hadn't had those planes on lakes, it would have been a very long freeze-up. As the bay is in walking distance it was a great occasion for everyone to see the plane. For many, it was the first plane they had seen since October. I had two letters from home and Christmas mail seems to be catching up now. This morning I had five patients to send out on the plane. As it was arriving earlier than anticipated I had to go whizzing round the village on my ski-doo at 8 o'clock and wake them up. After all that, we waited out on the ice for over for an hour before the plane landed. It is pretty cold these days hanging around outside; the temperature rarely rises above zero and if there is any wind, it feels even colder.

Sugluk: Joanesi Naluijuk carving soapstone

January 27th 1970

We are now getting planes fairly regularly. The plane is scheduled on a Monday but it is sometimes Friday before it gets here. A couple of weeks ago I went out to the plane with my ski-doo. As it was high tide the plane landed round the corner, which means it's a longer way round in order to avoid the water which overflows at the shoreline. Nelson didn't realise it was so deep and got stuck trying to get across on his ski-doo. I would have been terrified. I got my first box of fresh food from Blahey's which was very exciting but when I opened it I found a completely different order from what I had ordered. I couldn't understand it. I enquired around the village to see whether anyone had anything missing or anyone had my order by mistake but nobody had. Later I had a call from the nurses in POV asking if I had received my fresh food. They explained that my original order had sat in POV so long that they ate everything themselves and put in a new order for me but of course couldn't remember exactly what had been in it. Hence the different order. So that solved the mystery. Having not had any fresh food for so long I wanted to eat all those gorgeous vegetables and fruit at once! There were apples, pears, bananas, grapes, carrots, onions, Brussels sprouts, lettuce and cucumbers. What a feast! I had steak and Brussels sprouts that evening but I was so excited about the sprouts, I needn't have bothered with the steak.

I have had a couple of quiet weeks with baby clinics and immunisations and am preparing for Ora's visit. Jobie, an Eskimo from Wakeham Bay, who is a well known singer, has been singing with the group here, which includes three guitars and two violins. They are really good and keep swapping instruments all the time! I heard about Jobie while I was in George River.

Last Sunday we went for a ski-doo trip across the bay and up the mountains over the other side. It was a gorgeous day but about 20 below zero. My ski-doo was out of action so I sat on the back of Michelle's. The sun is getting stronger now and it gets dark between 3.30 and 4 p.m. We saw an amazing phenomenon later, with some reflection of the sun: there appeared to be three suns, one on each side of the 'real' sun then the reflections became rainbows. I have never seen anything like it. It was fantastic. I didn't have my camera with me but it is actually too cold to take photos at the moment anyway.

Last Monday an old lady fell and fractured her wrist while out fetching ice. I took an X-ray (it is so quick now I have everything set up) and bandaged it up and made arrangements for her to go out on the plane the following morning. As it happened, the weather was 'out' and the plane wouldn't be coming until Thursday. On Wednesday afternoon I had another very sick 10-month-old baby with pneumonia who I took in for the night. I had tried unsuccessfully to contact Dr Savoie but then managed to contact a doctor in Frobisher Bay over the radio. He was very reassuring and it was such a relief to have contact with another professional at a time like that. I waited for it to get light so that I could try and get a plane in for her. Her condition fluctuated all night and the poor little baby fought for breath. It is exhausting just watching and not being able to do more. Sadly, she died at 8 a.m.

I then had my morning clinic and in the afternoon waited to hear news of the plane. An hour beforehand I heard it was coming and had to rush round and collect up my seven patients I was sending out. The plane landed at 5 p.m., in the dark but without any trouble. Ora was on the plane and I have never been so glad to see anyone in my life! We spent the evening talking and catching up, it was wonderful. Later I took her over to the health centre and showed her my dark room. She was very impressed. She didn't yet know I had done all the X-rays, as Mary and I were going to surprise her on Friday, so Ora still thought we had 300 X-rays to do. We sat up late talking. The next day Mary and I led Ora on and asked her when she wanted to start the X-rays! We eventually put her out of her misery and presented her with the box of X-rays. It was a good joke. Ora was amazed and never suspected for a minute. I then had a very busy antenatal clinic.

The baby's funeral was at 12 p.m. and I went to it while Ora got lunch ready. It was about 30 below that day with a strong wind and below zero even inside the church. My nose froze up on the hill. Most of us go around with peeling noses anyway but it was rather painful. So, another funeral for the third of my 1969 babies. At least having Ora here was a comfort.

All afternoon Ora and I worked on paperwork and she went over some of the things she didn't have time to show me in September. We were there till 7 p.m. We came home to find it was 35 degrees in the trailer, the furnace must have gone off during the afternoon. We managed with difficulty to get it going again and after eating with our atigis on and the oven door open, by 8 o'clock the temperature had gone up to 50. We went to the mission for the film and found that everyone was having problems with their heating. Even oil freezes in severe cold. By now there was a gale and when we returned to the trailer at midnight it was 32 degrees inside - the furnace had stopped again. The water on the draining board had turned to ice but the water in the tank was still OK. We made a cup of tea that was luke-warm by the time it was poured out. My favourite chocolate cream biscuits were too hard to bite and our breath was visible in the cold air. Father Verspeek kindly came over to fix the furnace and it was 3 a.m. before we were happy that it was working again. And poor Ora, who hates the cold! By the next morning the temperature had gone up to 60 and by 12 p.m. it was a luxurious 68 degrees. We spent all afternoon doing paperwork and were almost surprised to find it was still warm when we went home. The wind was howling and it was 38 below zero outside.

On Monday we still had the X-rays of the babies I had saved until Ora's visit and I had called the first babies for 1.30 p.m. I was in the dark room and we had just done one X-ray when the power went off. I had to guess how long to leave the X-ray in the solution. It was 20 minutes before the power came on again and the 2 p.m. families were waiting by now so it was a bit crowded. After that everything went smoothly and we finished them all. It was pretty cold again in the trailer, with the storm but at least the furnace was still working.

I was up at 8.30 the next morning to hear about the plane as Ora would be leaving on it. Visibility was very poor, it was impossible to see across the bay, so it was a surprise to hear the plane circling overhead. We had a mad rush to get away, Ora had so much luggage (and the precious box of X-rays to be read by our TB consultant in Montreal) which we piled on to a sledge and started dragging it across the village. No-one could get a ski-doo started in that cold. The plane circled about six times and we thought it was going south again but suddenly we heard the revving of the engines so knew it had landed. We put our load into the snowmobile and set off for the plane. Not a single ski-doo was out! So that was Ora's visit, short and sweet. She is coming back again after the conference and we will also be going into Ivujivik again.

I shall be leaving for the annual conference next week. It will be in a luxury Swiss chalet-type hotel in the Laurentian Mountains. I must confess I feel badly in need of a break at the moment. This month has been especially draining with so many sleepless nights and losing three little babies. I am looking forward to meeting other nurses from our region and hearing about their experiences. We may get some skiing in the Laurentians too. It will feel like a holiday.

February 26th 1970 POVUNGNITUK (POV)

I left Sugluk on February 3rd and I could hardly wait another five minutes to get out! Things had suddenly caught up with me. I didn't care if we ended up in Cape Dorset or got stranded on an island somewhere, anywhere. I was sitting, in my atigi, by my phone ready to go at 8 a.m. The plane finally arrived at 10.30 and Lise and Joceline from POV were on board. As the plane had spent the night in POV they just came for the ride, which was nice for me. The temperature had fallen to 50 below during the night in POV so the engines were frozen and it took a long time getting away. They then had had to circle round over POV for an hour to warm the engines up. We left Sugluk about 11 o'clock, went up to Cape Dorset and Ivujivik, down the coast to POV and Port Harrison where we picked up the two nurses Lorraine and Monique, before landing in Great Whale at 7.30 p.m. Quite a trip in a DC3. The outside temperature was 45 below and not much warmer in the plane. The pilots daren't stop for too long anywhere because of the danger of the engines freezing again. There was a little Elsan type toilet in the back of the plane which felt like the outside temperature. I thought my bottom was going to freeze on the seat. We spent the day drinking coffee and eating biscuits. Conversation isn't easy in a noisy plane but it was so good to be together even though we didn't know each other. I had met Lise briefly of course when she came to fetch Evie at the lake but not the others. There were eight of us at Great Whale nursing station that night. We left for Montreal in the super Nordair jet which only took a couple of hours. I couldn't believe the size of Montreal after being so long in the 'bush'. I spent a couple of days with Ora in the office and went to the Royal Victoria Hospital where the psychiatrists wanted to learn more about the home environment of a young girl I had sent out some weeks ago. They were very interested to learn about all I could tell them. I hope it helped. We have Eskimo and Indian interpreters who work from the office in Montreal but they don't necessarily know all the details of each different settlement. I spent two nights with Claire and we had a lot to catch up on as usual.

On the Sunday we left for Ste Marguèrite where the conference was being held, at the Alpine Inn. We were housed in luxury chalets but had our meals in the main building. There were 36 of us in all but most are working on Indian reserves. The Indians seem more nomadic still and it must be a nightmare keeping up with their immunisations and X-rays. They also seem to have more alcohol problems which the Eskimos don't. I never realised that our Montreal office covered such a large area. Of course Quebec province IS large. We had lectures on antibiotics, skin diseases, TB, congenital dislocation of the hip (a particular problem with Indians who tend to bind their babies flat to sleep) and we had a three hour discussion on immunisations. Five years ago, that would have been a three hour discussion on infectious diseases but times are changing rapidly. A few years ago measles nearly wiped out whole populations of Eskimos. We also had hours on administration; there are so many forms to fill out these days as well as writing medical records. Louisette and I went skiing a few times; the piste is lit up at night. The five days went very quickly and I feel I learned a lot. Dr Savoie and Pauline Laurin held a cocktail party for everyone on the last evening.

I had to go to the dentist in Montreal and he wanted to extract a wisdom tooth that was lying horizontal in the jaw. Although it wasn't causing any problem at the time, it would be very awkward and expensive if I had to be evacuated with it in the middle of the break-up so Mlle Laurin advised me to have it done now. I had a local anaesthetic and stitches so had to take five days off sick until the stitches came out.

March 14th 1970
SUGLUK

Lise had taken a week's holiday after the conference so we travelled north together on March 1st on the 8 a.m. flight from Montreal to Great Whale. Dr Bernstein, a physician and Dr Perron, a paediatrician were also on that flight for their annual visits to our settlements. Dr Perron was to join me on the Monday to start in Sugluk. I went up to POV to wait for the next plane into Sugluk. Johnny May had a private charter going into Sugluk the next morning and I was hoping to go on that. It was lovely to see him again. (Memories of George River!) Unfortunately there wasn't enough room so I had to wait for Monday's scheduled flight. I enjoyed my weekend in POV and was back here in Sugluk on the Tuesday after a month away. Dr Perron and M. Gervais, who is our maintenance supervisor, both came up the same day so I had two men to cook for as well as all the work! Actually they were very good and we took it in turns to cook so everything went well. They stayed a week and Dr Perron examined all 180 children. He was very sweet with the children and I learned a lot from him. The way to approach a toddler is via his shoes (kamiks or boots here!) Small children respond to praise of their footwear. He left me with 120 prescriptions to dish out (mainly antibiotics for otitis and bronchitis) as well as all the records to write up so it was pretty hectic. The prescriptions took me three days to make up and virtually finished my stock.

M. Gervais got my ski-doo in working order again so that is good. He told me that they are sending up two brand new trailers this summer. Back-to-back they will make a new clinic and storage area. It sounds fantastic and I can't wait to get it all set up. I am also getting a 'play cat' which is more solid than a ski-doo and is an all-terrain vehicle so I shall be able to use it all the year round.

This month is going by really quickly. Soon it will be April and my parents will be on their way here.

Sugluk village

Povungnituk (POV): demonstration igloo

April 5th 1970

Dr Simard, the physician, came the following week, to examine all the adults. He arrived on the Monday (16th March) and as there were only 100 adults to see he decided to try and see them all in three days so he could get back to Great Whale and finish the 800 he still had to examine there, so we worked late every evening and finished on Thursday morning. I couldn't help being amused by the fact that he sat there puffing away whilst advising patients to stop smoking! What with TB and bronchitis, most of the population has chest problems.

I had chartered a plane for Dr Simard for Thursday afternoon. On the Wednesday evening Ora radiosed me from Great Whale and asked, as I was chartering that plane, could I go into Ivujivik for ten days to do the X-rays and immunisations? She wasn't going to have time to come with me but she would join me back here afterwards. That really was a bit of a panic, collecting everything together at such short notice! I managed to pack up the X-ray equipment, dark tent, all the records and vaccines which totalled 16 pieces of luggage and weighed over 500 pounds. So I left with Dr Simard on the Thursday and they dropped me off in Ivujivik first. The plane landed just in time as there was a storm brewing; another half-hour and we would have been unable to land.

Steve met me and helped me take all the X-ray equipment over to the school. He invited me to supper and was really pleased to see me as he had a lot to tell me and ask me. I was also very pleased to see him, he is so kind, devoted and reliable. As well as teaching he has the lay dispensing to do. I was also very happy to be back in Ivujivik again. I do love these small places where the people are still unspoiled. Later, Steve helped me with my luggage over to the health centre in the storm. Every step was an extraordinary effort, with the howling, biting wind blowing snow into our faces, taking our breath away. A real struggle against the elements. This really gave me some insight into what Scott must have experienced on his expeditions. How exhausting just this short walk across the village with a box of dehydrated food was! What must it have been like for Scott, over a much longer period and much longer distances?

It was fun to be 'camping out' again in the health centre. There is now a 75 gallon water tank with a tap on it, which is an improvement on the two buckets Ora and I had last time. There is also a new stove. With the storm, the temperature dropped to 30 inside so even in my Arctic sleeping bag I was a bit cold in the night. The next night I turned the stove up before I went to bed and woke later in a sweltering 90 degrees! That was far worse. I would always rather be too cold than too hot.

Steve and Sarah, the Eskimo interpreter, helped me with the X-rays. I set up all the equipment on Friday morning and was relieved to find everything in working order. We managed to take 35 X-rays that first day. I saved the developing until later. It was great fun being back in the X-ray business again! I worked until midnight developing and on Saturday we did another 56 X-rays. Steve and I were invited to supper with Nicole and Réal, a very nice young French Canadian couple, teachers with the provincial government. We had a lovely meal and talked late into the night. On Sunday I slept late and then went over to the school to finish the developing. On Monday school was cancelled as we still had the final X-rays to do. The children thought it was wonderful and wanted to help. They were happy to run around fetching different families to come for their X-rays. There was a plane that day and Rona Williams was on it, on her way south to have her baby. I had also run short of vaccines and had got a message to Elizabeth (who was standing in for me while I was away) asking her to send them to me with Rona. Having finished the X-rays, I now had plenty of time in a week to do all the medicals and immunisations. I called people by family and combined medicals and immunisations to save them all coming out twice. Children were once again delighted to run around fetching families. The last job I still had to do was getting the schoolchildren to brush their teeth with special fluoride toothpaste. It is quite complicated and takes about ten minutes for each child as it is important to stress they mustn't swallow it. It was easier for me to brush the teeth of the little ones myself then take groups of two or three together and explain and supervise them. I could take the older children in groups of four. This is going to be an annual event and was explained to us at the conference. So I shall have 80 children in Sugluk to do when I get back.

On Good Friday I went for a long walk with Réal and Nicole. We climbed up the rocks behind the village, walked right round to where we could see the ice where the Hudson Bay meets the Hudson Strait. What an amazing sight! Huge boulders of ice are piled up along the shore. We went down to the shore and back to the other side of the village. Ivujivik means 'the place where the ice piles up' and I can see why. We had supper with Steve and he showed us his slides of Greenland where he spent a couple of months on holiday. My plans to work in Greenland seem to have become substituted by the Canadian Arctic but who knows? I may get there yet.

Ivujivik Eskimos show films several times a week, they order them through the co-op. One night we saw 'Sinbad's Seven Voyages', a real 'Tarzan' type film which they loved, despite the fact that the projector broke down 11 times. On Saturday they had a 'Western', which started with reel one, followed by reel three, reel two and then reel three again. Reel four was missing so we never found out what happened at the end. This did not detract from their enjoyment at all.

On Sunday (Easter Day) I borrowed Steve's ski-doo and went down to look at the ice again. I managed to get the ski-doo stuck in ice and couldn't turn it round. There was a huge chunk of ice caught between the skis. I walked a couple of miles back to the village to find Saima, a very helpful Eskimo, who came back with me and freed it with an axe. Later on I accompanied Steve and some of the schoolchildren on a walk around the hills. Then I went to church and the evening finished with a dance. The usual 15 minute square dances. On Monday I had to pack up all my equipment ready to leave for Sugluk. I was still packing when I heard the plane circling overhead! It was a mad rush to get down to the plane and the pilot all but left without me. Ora was on the plane and it was lovely to see her again.

When we arrived in Sugluk Father Verspeek met us and broke the news that while I was away my furnace had stopped one night, resulting in frozen pipes and a burst water pump, which he had welded. Poor Father Verspeek must have been there all day, he had cleared up all the mess and the temperature was already up to 50 degrees by the time we arrived.

On Wednesday, not only did two babies have convulsions but Elizabeth's baby had some sort of episode and stopped breathing. Elizabeth thought it was a missed cot death and she was naturally very worried. On Thursday I chartered a plane for one of the Eskimo babies who continued to convulse and Elizabeth escorted this baby and took her own baby with her. Montreal called and asked as I was chartering the plane, could I send four patients out who had hospital appointments. I managed to find three of them and hurriedly wrote up their records with 45 minutes notice. The fourth will have to wait till the next plane. Ora and I spent most of Saturday doing paperwork but we took Sunday off.

On the Sunday afternoon we went on a ski-doo trip with Father Verspeek, about four or five miles down the bay where there is a patch of open water. We found a group of Eskimos collecting mussels at the low tide. It was a lovely sunny day. My drive belt broke on the way back and once more I had to abandon my ski-doo and get a lift with Father Verspeek. On Monday afternoon Ora left for Port Harrison.

At 2.30 a.m. on Tuesday I was called for a delivery. It was one I had been expecting and it was a beautiful delivery of a seven pound baby boy at 4.30. I caught up on some paperwork and the morning clinic was not too busy. At 12.00, much to my surprise, I had a radio call from my parents to say they were already in Montreal. This was a big surprise as I didn't think they were leaving for a few days. I am very excited and dying to see them.

Ivujivik: the ice piled up

CHAPTER 6
MY PARENTS' VISIT

AT THIS POINT I INCLUDE MY FATHER'S
DIARY WHICH COVERS APRIL 6th to 29th 1970. I had
no idea he had written a diary and only discovered it in
2003. Obviously I didn't write to my parents during that
time, so this fills the gap.

Monday April 6th

*We left home on a raw grey day with some snow about. Took train to
Woking and taxi to Heathrow. We had time to wait and watched the
mixture of nationalities going about. We were surprised to walk straight
from the airport building into the jet. The 707 was most smooth and
comfortable though Frances held my hand during take-off! Lunch and tea on
the plane were first rate, hot dishes really hot and dainty fresh sandwiches at
tea. Bright sunshine all the way and lovely views of icy mountains and a
frozen sea.*

*Claire met us at the airport and took us to her flat. When John came
in we had dinner by candlelight.*

Tuesday April 7th

*Sunny all day but cold. A depressing start to the day when Claire
found out that the Wednesday plane we planned to take to Great Whale had
already gone early this morning so it appeared we could not leave till NEXT
Tuesday which would mean we wouldn't see Anne for two weeks! After all*

the money she had sent us, she would only have us for one week. However, Claire spent a whole morning on the phone, including getting in touch with Anne herself and discovered we could get to Timmins by way of Toronto and from there to Povungnituk which is only an hour's flight from Sugluk. Great relief!

Wednesday April 8th

We said Au Revoir to Claire and left Montreal at 12.15 on a cold grey morning. Our jet this time was a DC9 which took us very smoothly into bright sun over miles of farm land to Toronto. A nice hot lunch on board although the flight was less than an hour. At 3.10 we left Toronto in a Viscount (prop) for Timmins, getting there at 4.50. Timmins airport consists of a wooden hut and a runway surrounded by a waste of snow and silver birch. Timmins town is nearly ten miles away and is a prosperous mushroom town depending on copper mining. We booked in at the Empire Hotel which was surprisingly plushy, with bath and television attached to our bedroom.

At the air terminal we heard a man asking for a charter plane from POV to Sugluk tomorrow so chipped in and arranged to join him.

Thursday April 9th

Left Timmins at 7 a.m. in a twin engine plane and flew at 8,000 ft. over stunted forests to Moosonee. Landed on a frozen lake. We carried twelve passengers of whom seven stayed there. One was Mlle Rousseau, a nursing superintendent who was going elsewhere but looked like being stuck because of bad weather.

In the airport building, was a can of snow being melted on a stove for drinking water.

The pilot, Steve Enneke, knew Anne and said he had flown her several times. Five of us boarded the plane after twenty minutes and were dished out with lunch packs (sandwiches, egg, cheese and fruit) "...To last all day".

11 a.m. Landed at Great Whale but stayed only ten minutes. Met by a small crowd of Eskimos and several came on board. No trees now.

1 p.m. Stopped briefly at Port Harrison, unloaded a lot of cargo and more Eskimos came aboard. Ora Babcock came aboard and introduced herself. Bright sunshine.

2.30 We landed at POV. Looked out for a few minutes but the wind was so icy I soon got back in again.

3.50 Arrived Sugluk, landing on the bay. A beautiful hilly village after all the desolate flatness we have seen since Timmins. Anne met us on a ski-doo and we rode with the luggage in a snowmobile. Very impressed by her luxurious house. Saw over her health centre.

Friday April 10th

Anne went off to work at 9.00 and we attempted to make toast for breakfast but found there was a power cut. This of course meant there was no water and the heating was off. However it came on again in half an hour and all was well.

A beautiful sunny morning and we went out for a walk but after a few hundred yards ears and noses were beginning to nip and we came in again. Sun glasses are essential in the glare from the snow. The snow is beautifully clean and crisp.

After tea Anne took us to the co-op and "The Bay" and we called on Lorenzo who lives in a fascinating very modern triangular house. Anne developed X-rays till 11 p.m.

Saturday April 11th

I walked with Anne to the top of the hill to the south and took photographs. Then we all visited Chris Williams, the Anglican minister and his four-year-old son. His wife was away in Toronto having a baby. Chris is from Manchester. He was busy baking bread.

Then we called on the two teachers Joan and Nelson Richards, both Canadian. We met Sinclair Colleymore, an administrator for the federal government. At night we went to a cinema show at the house of Mike Banks (teacher). The film was a western and kept breaking, the projector also gave trouble.

Sunday April 12th

Anne took me and Mike took Frances on ski-doos about five miles out on the bay. We came to fast running water which never freezes. Saw a seal. Beautiful snow and ice formations.

Monday April 13th

Went to the Bay for stamps but was told "…only on Fridays". Walked round the village and up the hill with Frances.

The plane came in at 3.30 and we all went down in the snowmobile to meet it.

Seal liver for supper. Played Scrabble with Anne.

Tuesday April 14th

Much colder after snow in the night. Frances and I went down to Chris Williams and bought some small carvings. After lunch Anne had a baby clinic and we took some pictures. Terry and Vera came to supper.

Wednesday April 15th

Another brilliant day with no wind. Took some little walks and photographed the church. Went to supper with Nelson and Joan and her father (Mr McDonnand). They had a projector and we saw slides of theirs and Anne's. After that we went to a dance. Very noisy and crowded and disorganised. A sort of square dance to something like Scottish music. The band was one fiddle, one accordion, two spoons and a washboard. Eskimos very energetic.

Father Verspeek returned from a ski-doo trip to Wakeham Bay.

Thursday April 16th

Bright sun again but a sharp wind. We went to see Tivi carving a lump of stone outside his house. He is one of the best carvers in the village. Called in at the co-op and bought a small carving of a seal and baby. Bought an Eskimo doll for Suzie.

In the afternoon we went to the junior school and saw Joan's dancing class and Mike's gymnasts. After supper to a musical evening in Father Verspeek's hall. Anne took her tape recorder.

Friday April 17th

We went to the Bay for stamps, had a look round the co-op and then walked down to the shore. In the evening we went to Father Verspeek's cinema show, had coffee after and stayed very late talking.

Sugluk: my parents with Father Verspeek (standing left)

Saturday April 18th

We all got up late and then walked out on the fjord in the direction of the Hudson Strait. Very exhilarating especially coming back when we faced the wind. After lunch Anne and I called on Lucien who showed us round the power house and the garages.

Anne was called out to a confinement after tea and we had supper without her. Joan, Nelson and Don came in about 9.00 and stayed for a cup of tea. They had been out on ski-doos and had shot a brace of ptarmigan.

Sunday April 19th

We rose very late to find a strong wind whipping the surface off the snow. Anne came in about noon, having spent the night at the clinic. Snow blowing all day. When Anne had had a bath and a meal we played scrabble all afternoon. The heating of the house was far too high and Anne rang Father Verspeek who came over and diagnosed penetrating wind getting into the thermostat.

We all went to church, quite a number of Eskimos there and Mr McDonnand gave the sermon. After church we went for tea and cake at Nelson and Joan's. Joan lent me an atigi. Still blowing hard at midnight.. Caribou steak for supper. The woman last night had her baby at 8.15 p.m. and went home in a blizzard at 9 a.m.

Monday April 20th

60 m.p.h. gale blew all night, blowing clouds of fine snow. Started to go out after breakfast but retired when I felt the force of the wind. At midday it abated. Don called at 1.30 after seeing the clinic and I walked down with him to the store. At 3.00 Anne expected the snowmobile to take her to the plane but at 4.30 Terry phoned to say the pilot was lost near Deception Bay. At 5 p.m. we saw the snowmobile on the shore and heard a plane. Anne and I went out and found the snowmobile broken down so she set off to walk but I came back as all the snow had been blown off the bay leaving it a sheet of ice. Soon after she returned with Father Verspeek, the plane hadn't landed after all. Don and Chris, who had expected to be on it were unable to go. Played Scrabble, Anne won.

Tuesday April 21st

Fine and sunny, wind gone. Called on Father Verspeek and had coffee and a talk. He gave me a biscuit tin and I got some peaty soil, thawed it out and sowed cress. The first sowing on wadding was a failure. (? medicated)

A plane came in about noon and Frances and I walked out to see it. The bare ice was now covered with snow again. Rode home in snowmobile.

Looked in at co-op and saw Michelle who said we could see her school.

After supper a George River Eskimo called Mark came visiting. He had coffee with us and played Scrabble!

Wednesday April 22nd

Anne was called out at 6.30 a.m. to a sick baby.

We went to the kindergarten where Madonne had seven infants. Later we saw the new provincial school at the invitation of Michelle.

Bought a carving of a man with a fish on his back. Played Scrabble.

Thursday April 23rd

Fine and sunny. After an early lunch we set off for Sugluk Island, about six miles in the Hudson Strait. Father Verspeek took me on the back of his ski-doo and Frances in a "side car" trailer. Anne rode her own machine. We walked on the island, saw the remains of early stone houses and many bones including the skull of a whale. Took photos by a large clump of blue ice.

On our return we went to the running water at the other end of the fjord. Father Verspeek collected and ate mussels. We had coffee at his house and later he came to supper. (Steak).

Friday April 24th

Frances and I went to the Bay then watched stone carvers at work. Father Verspeek gave us a private slide show at night.

Saturday April 25th

Anne was called out at 9.30 to a baby which didn't arrive by 2.00. Quick lunch and out again 2.30 for half an hour. During all this time she and I kept a game of Scrabble going. She went out again at 4.00 and at 7.00. Elizabeth Banks came in for a few minutes.

Anne cooked a delicious Arctic char for supper and went out again to her expectant Eskimo.

Sunday April 26th

Baby born at midnight. Anne out all night and came in at 10.30.

A little snow during the night. We rose late, shortly before Anne came in. At 12.00 we were invited to dinner with Madonne and Lorenzo the provincial administrator, and their three lively children, Caroline (6) and twins Patrice and Natalie (2½). Father Verspeek was there too. Excellent dinner.

Played Scrabble with Anne and had more Arctic char for supper. Then to Mike and Elizabeth Banks for drinks. Played family bridge till after midnight then had tea and cake.

Eskimo names:

Christian names: Lukasi, Paulusi, Adamie, Thomasie, Josepi, Angutigirk, Kadyulik, Matthewsie, Putulik.

Surnames: Ainalik, Ilisituk, Kiatainak, Komak, Kupirkaluk, Okituk, Papigatuk, Saviadjuk, Takrik, Yuyusi.

Frances is to take a three week old Eskimo baby from here to Great Whale. The baby is jaundiced and as its escort her fare will be paid by the government.

Monday April 27th

Cold grey day. We returned Joan's atigi and said goodbye to her and Nelson. Bought two more small carvings at the co-op. Got 25% off "...for the nurse".

After lunch we finished last night's game of Scrabble. When the plane was due we collected our luggage and went to the clinic where we met baby

Putulik Angutigirk and his mother, who came down to the plane. After goodbyes we left at 5.20 p.m. Soon ran into sunshine and were in POV in an hour. The two POV nurses met us and a snowmobile took us to the nursing station. An Eskimo woman took charge of the baby.

The two French speaking nurses showed us round the large house and clinic and walked us round the settlement. One of them had given up her very comfortable bedroom for us. They fed us enormous steaks which we were unable to finish.

Tuesday April 28th

The plane left POV for Great Whale at 9.30 and during the flight the pilot told us that the Nordair for Montreal was running two hours late. Did we want to catch it? We said yes and he radioed to see if seats were available. He also radioed the Great Whale nurse to make arrangements for Putulik to travel with us. At Great Whale the baby was taken off our hands, changed and fed and brought back to our jet (a 707) at 2 p.m. At Montreal airport two SAVI nurses took Putulik and we rang Claire and took a taxi to her place.

Friday May 1st

We took two taxis to the docks, John and Claire came on board the Empress of Canada, had a drink and looked round the ship.

Saturday May 2nd

The ship sailed at dawn and we cruised smoothly all day down the St. Lawrence River.

May 7th 1970

It was lovely having my parents for almost three weeks but I missed them after they had gone. I gathered from Lise in POV that they enjoyed their visit too. I wonder what sort of crossing they are having; I hope they are not having hurricane-force gales as we are.

One evening, about a week ago, several of us left for the island where Ruth's ski-doo had been abandoned. Two people broke down on the way and as usual, I was far behind the others. About four miles out of the village my belt gave out so there was absolutely nothing I could do except leave my ski-doo there and start walking home. After a mile or so I could see what looked like small figures running in and out of the oil drums. I was beginning to think it was either some kind of mirage in the white desert or I was hallucinating with snow blindness. As I got nearer, I realised it was Father Verspeek with his jeep. He had seen us set out and decided to follow but ran into deep snow and couldn't get out. We laughed at each other's misfortune and walked back together to the village. It was a beautiful warm evening with temperatures in the 30s.

On Saturday May 2nd it was the 300th anniversary of the Hudson's Bay Company and of course that had to be celebrated. In the afternoon Terry went up into the loft of the Bay and for an hour or so threw out balloons and sweets alternately so that the children were jumping for balloons one minute and grovelling for sweets the next. It was very windy and balloons went high. The children loved the excitement.

On Monday I discovered two children with chickenpox, both visiting from Wakeham Bay. They have an epidemic there so I can expect one here in two or three weeks. I have sent for a good supply of Calamine lotion.

On Tuesday I was called for little Kalingo who is five, with suspected appendicitis. I started him on adult doses of antibiotics as I couldn't intervene in any other way. I contacted Dr Savoie who promised to get a plane in for me the next day. This was a real emergency and I would have to escort this child myself. I was woken early the next morning by a plane circling overhead and thought I must be dreaming. It landed and I rushed down to see what it was and where it was going. It was a Beech from Chimo on an errand for the co-op and the pilot planned to leave as soon as the wind had died down a bit. I contacted Dr Savoie who told me I must charter the plane and take Kalingo to Frobisher Bay hospital. I informed the pilot who agreed to take us as soon as possible. Medical emergencies always have priority over other trips. We were packed and ready to leave at a moment's notice but the wind soon became gale-force and it was clear we were in for one of our storms. Luckily Kalingo was stable. Last night, at midnight I was called out for Josephie who had a finger crushed by a door that was blown back on his hand. The first joint was almost severed so all I could do was splint and dress it and give him penicillin. He will have to come with us to Frobisher Bay where they will probably have to amputate. So he is also ready to leave at a moment's notice. At 6.30 this morning I was woken for a delivery which went well. This baby was to be adopted by another family. Sometimes it is prearranged that a particular baby is destined for adoption. It often seems to be to replace a death but not necessarily of a baby.

The storm has been raging all day, the worst we have ever had. Father Verspeek reckoned that the wind has been about 100 miles an hour. He came in for a little while this afternoon to sit with mother and baby so that Susie (who has now taken over from Mary as my interpreter) and I could go and visit the two patients. Just before we went out Father Verspeek told us about a couple of girls in POV who walked through their village in a similar storm and not being able to see where they were, probably thought they were lost and carried on past the village. They were found dead of exposure the next day, not far from home. A cautionary tale. Susie and I went out into the storm and we could hardly see where we were going in the blizzard so we made our way through the village on our hands and knees, hanging on to each other as we went. Once again I was reminded of Scott's expeditions. Little Kalingo's condition was still stable, I just pray that he can hold on and his appendix won't rupture. Josephie's finger was comfortable so that was a relief. It is now 6 p.m. and I am once again playing the waiting game. I have sent mother and baby on their separate ways.

May 17th 1970

Ten days later! On the Friday (the day after I last wrote) the weather was clear and it looked hopeful. I was having a very hectic morning clinic when I had a message to say that the plane would be leaving at 10.30. I was fully dressed, ready to go and tried to fit in as many patients as possible in those final minutes before abandoning the clinic. However, after half an hour, I could see from the window that they appeared to be having engine trouble so I removed my atigi and managed to see all the patients. At 12 p.m. we set off in the snowmobile for the plane. We spent another half an hour on the ice with one engine still playing up, so it was 1 o'clock before we finally took off. Little Kalingo was very brave, it was his first time away from home and he shed a few tears as he clutched a little toy plane. We hit a patch of thick fog and had to descend to about 500 feet. I really thought we were going to have to land on the Hudson Strait. Luckily things improved and we landed safely in Frobisher Bay at 2.30 p.m. A car (!) from the hospital came to pick us up and we were seen straightaway. Both my patients were admitted immediately. Kalingo's appendicitis had subsided with antibiotics but he was to be sent to Montreal for appendicectomy. Josephie was taken straight to theatre where his finger was examined. Apparently it was already healing well and they didn't think it would need amputating. They would keep him under observation. I was very thankful about both my patients after those rather anxious few days with little sleep.

After leaving my patients in expert care I had to make arrangements to spend the night there as the pilot was not returning to Sugluk that day. It is a huge hospital with six or seven doctors and fourteen nurses. Everyone was very friendly. Marlene Jacobs is the nurse in charge and a real character. I hadn't been there five minutes before she had fixed me up with a date for the evening! I called Montreal to let them know where I was and I was told to charter the plane back to Sugluk as soon as possible. I had half hoped I might be able to escort Kalingo to Montreal. The weather was fast closing in by now so I could relax in Frobisher Bay with no responsibilities. After supper in the hospital canteen I was taken to my lodgings, sharing a flat with Diana, a nurse on her way up to Igloolik. Later Thorley and Witold, our two dates, came to take us out. They both work in the Nordair office. We went to the Legion club where we danced and drank to 'mod' music, (as opposed to Eskimo music). Later we went to their place and talked until 3.30 a.m., by which time it was light. I was possibly leaving at 5, weather permitting of course. I woke at 9 o'clock and learned that we wouldn't be leaving before the afternoon. At 12 o'clock I left Diana still sleeping and called the hospital to ask them to send a car (what luxury!) to pick me up to go for lunch. I talked to two young doctors, Fernando and Michel, who had only arrived the week before. It was such fun to meet new people. In the afternoon Fernando, Michel and I took one of the hospital jeeps and drove to Apex, a village three miles from Frobisher, with a population of 500 Eskimos. The weather was terrible, temperature about 40 and slush everywhere. We had a look around the Hudson's Bay store, went back to Frobisher and chatted for a while. By now it was supper time. I tried to contact the pilot to see what was happening but he was nowhere to be found. I called the met. office who told me it was 'zero zero' in Sugluk. Next weather report 5 a.m. So I could relax for another night! Thorley and Witold came round for a chat. They are both young and have spent three years at university, one in engineering and the other in arts. Witold is Polish and speaks four languages. It seems such a waste that two brainy young people should be writing out tickets all day. They don't really know what to do with their lives.

I woke about 11 o'clock the next morning, weather 'closed-in' everywhere, so I anticipated another day in Frobisher Bay. After lunch I joined Michel and Fernando and showed them some of my slides, (I always take some around with me) which they enjoyed. We stayed at the hospital after supper because Michel was on call and expecting a patient who had a 'crack' in his eye. We were all dying to see this man with a cracked eye but he never turned up. It will remain a mystery. Later Michel and I went on our own to see the film 'The pride of Miss Jean Brody', as Fernando had seen it and Diana wanted to phone her mother. It was excellent. Maggie Smith won an Oscar with it. We came home, had a coffee and a chat and I went to bed wondering if I would really be leaving at 5 a.m.

I was called at 8.30 on Monday and told we would be leaving at 9. I dressed quickly and a car came to pick me up and take me to the airport. Weather reports were still pretty bad everywhere and it was impossible to contact Sugluk at all. In all there were five planes grounded at Frobisher and one had been there since the Wednesday. My pilot had already passed his dateline to be back in Chimo for his plane check-up and officially he should have been heading straight back there. Weather was clear in Deception Bay and if it should turn bad between Frobisher and Deception, we would go to Koartak and back to Chimo. A mystery trip! We eventually took off at 11.30. I was in the mood for adventure. By the time we had crossed the strait, visibility improved and we landed in Sugluk without any adventure. I was rather disappointed, I must confess. I had really enjoyed my little holiday in Frobisher Bay and it was particularly refreshing to meet new people. It is a real little town with taxis, a hairdresser, psychedelic club, cinema, Hudson's Bay store, Co-op, liquor store (alcohol), post office, bank, sweet shop and a Scottish knitwear shop. I even saw some road signs and bus stops. There are over a thousand Eskimos and several hundred white people there.

Meanwhile, in Sugluk, they had had several feet of snow. It had snowed solidly for three days with gales from the north which is most unusual. Now the snow has built up on the front of my house and it was halfway up the front door till Father Verspeek dug it out a bit. It is now up to the front step and I have to be careful coming out otherwise I sink up to my waist in snow. Of course, now it is milder the snow is soft. It takes ages getting anywhere in this deep snow. The weather closed in again as soon as I got back. I was very lucky to get Kalingo and Josephie safely to hospital.

Father Verspeek took over in my absence and had been really busy. He had a delivery on the Saturday which had been a bit complicated, had some suturing to do and a couple of cases of pneumonia. He is very capable and I'm always confident to leave him in charge. I suspect he enjoyed it too. Memories of the 'good old days'.

At the moment temperatures are in the 30s on the whole, though it can drop to zero again. It stays light until almost 11 p.m. but never gets really dark. It is daylight again at 2.30 a.m.

The day I got back, Mary's 14-year-old brother and another man had been missing for three days. They went ptarmigan hunting on the Saturday and search parties were out looking for them. Their ski-doo ran out of petrol between here and Deception Bay and they walked all Saturday evening, Saturday night, Sunday and Sunday night and were eventually picked up on Monday afternoon. They must have been exhausted. I was expecting them to come down with pneumonia but as I haven't seen them, presumably they are OK. An R.A.F. plane was out yesterday, looking for a missing plane somewhere between Chimo and Frobisher. I haven't heard any news of that yet.

There are plenty of snow buntings about at the moment so spring is really in the air. It is fun to see them flitting over the snow. They are still white but will change colour when the snow melts. It seems strange to have birds and no trees.

My ski-doo is buried under three feet of snow and if the shovel weren't buried under six feet, I could dig it out.

Yesterday a little two-year-old girl came to me with a crushed finger. I shall see how it looks tomorrow and I may have to send her out.

CHAPTER 7
CHICKENPOX INTERLUDE

June 24th 1970
ST MARY'S HOSPITAL TIMMINS

A lot has happened this last month. On Monday 25th May I had to evacuate a sick baby and escorted him myself as I had a throat infection which was not responding to treatment. I was hoping to be back on the Thursday so took just enough things for three days. We spent a night at Port Harrison and I was able to see their nursing station. The following day I was in Montreal, dressed in all my winter clothes and the temperatures were in the 90s! Claire was away and everyone at the office was in conference until 5 p.m. I had a box of X-rays from POV to deliver there. As I couldn't take my atigi off all afternoon I was really suffering with the heat. Eventually I went to the office, saw Ora and stayed for a chat. Then I stayed in the Laurentian Hotel which was paid for out of travel expenses. I was so relieved to undress and have a bath and put on something cooler. Ora came down to the hotel later and we went to see the film 'MASH' which was very funny. The next day I went to see a doctor who did some blood tests and gave me stronger antibiotics. That evening I managed to track down Inge, one of my Danish friends whom I knew was in Montreal for a year. It was fun to be speaking Danish again and we went to see a Danish film that night.

On the Wednesday, I left with Ora who was going to Great Whale. We travelled via Timmins this time - my first time there. We booked into the Empire Hotel. It was almost 90 degrees in Timmins but not humid like in Montreal. In the evening Ora had some business up at the hospital so I went with her. We had some discussions with Mme Gagnon, the supervisor, about evacuating patients. She also showed us round the hospital. We were very impressed with this modern 300 bed hospital. Timmins has only existed for 60 years. It is a mining town with a population of about 30,000.

We left at 7.30 the next morning and were in Great Whale at 11 o'clock having stopped in Moosonee and Fort George on the way. As the break-up had already started in POV, I had to stay in Great Whale until the Monday for the flight back to Sugluk. Connie and Alice, two English Canadians, are the new nurses in Great Whale. I had only met them briefly when passing through before. They are both very nice and seem good fun. It is their first time in the Arctic. There was no snow left and temperatures were in the 60s. Saturday was Ora's birthday so Daisy, the Eskimo interpreter and I went down to the co-op to choose a nice carving for her. A glorious sunset at 10 p.m. so I took some photos.

On the Saturday, to my horror, I found a couple of suspicious looking blisters and my immediate thought was that it was chickenpox! My heart sank as that would mean I would not be able to return to Sugluk on Monday. I covered them up again and hoped perhaps they would disappear. I didn't say a word to anyone but as the day went on I began to feel increasingly unwell and eventually had to 'confess'. Ora said, "I knew you weren't yourself," and she wasn't surprised. However, if I could just spend a few days in bed at Great Whale, I hoped I might get back to Sugluk the following week, in time before the break-up. After a few days, by now covered in Chickenpox and unable to sleep because of the irritation, I was getting worse instead of better. Ora was worried and called Dr Savoie who told her to get me out to hospital on the next plane as it was possible that there were complications which could lead to encephalitis. Ora came with me to Timmins the following day. Little did I know I would be back there as a patient a week later! I was admitted to Emergency on a trolley as there were no beds available. I didn't care as long as I could lie down. Later that evening I was taken to an isolation room on a men's medical ward. The doctor explained that I had a generalised infection including peritonitis, which sometimes happens with adults with chickenpox. They also took samples to make sure it wasn't smallpox. I was only allowed fluids for a couple of days. I did not expect to be here for over two weeks and the worst problem has been boredom as I'm not allowed out of the room and no-one is allowed in without 'gowning up'. In desperation I hired a television last week. Paying for it was an extraordinary performance! While one of the nurses stood in the doorway, with an open envelope, I had to drop the money into it without touching the envelope, then the money had to be fumigated before it could be handed over to the TV rental people. You would have thought I had smallpox! I have had a few visitors: one little old man who is a diabetic patient on the ward, comes and stands in the corridor (I'm allowed to keep the door open) to talk to me several times a day, he knows he can't come into the room. He is French Canadian and thankful to find someone who can speak French. One Sunday Lorraine was on her way back to Port Harrison and she came to visit. Last Sunday the cathedral sent me some flowers which I thought was a lovely gesture. Apparently they do this when outsiders are in Timmins hospital. Two of the ministers have also been to see me and then, later on that Sunday a friend of Chris Williams who had been visiting in Sugluk, on his way home, heard my name on the prayer list at the cathedral and came to see me. Montreal have been phoning me every day from the office too, which is nice. I have a phone in my room. Apparently Father Verspeek is managing to hold the fort in Sugluk while I'm stuck here.

June 28th 1970
MONTREAL.

At last they let me out yesterday! Two and a half weeks in the same room is an experience not to be repeated. Every day seemed longer than the last. I was let out at 11 a.m. and had to wait until 12.30 while they fumigated my room, before I could get dressed and pack up my belongings. One of the men on the ward asked me if I was the one with smallpox! Not surprising with all the precautions. I had my last meal with paper plates and plastic cutlery. Mrs Baxter, one of the nurses, is Spanish and she invited me to spend the afternoon at her house while I was waiting for the plane. She was very kind to me and it was fun speaking Spanish again too. She was interested to see some of my slides and it was a lovely afternoon back in 'civilisation.' It was 80 degrees in Timmins but only 59 here in Montreal.

July 7th 1970
GREAT WHALE RIVER

After almost a week's convalescence in Montreal, I came up to Great Whale. I pleaded with the office to let me fly to Great Whale on the Friday as I was so bored in Montreal. I promised I would not do any work before Monday when my sick certificate ran out. (Canadians are very strict about not working if officially off sick). It was a very bumpy flight, even in the jet. We went through bumpy clouds until about half an hour out of Great Whale. The weather has been beautiful all week and we have been down to the beach most evenings to watch the sunset. We have lit fires on the rocks and stayed down there chatting to various people until well after dark. There are two groups of archeologists, three groups of anthropologists, a group of biologists and a few transient doctors and dentists here at the moment so it is pretty busy. On Sunday we watched the archeologists hard at work and they showed us some of their findings. They have found some ancient remains of houses, flint chippings, arrow heads, a knife and some charcoal remains dating back over a thousand years. As yet they haven't found any bones.

Dr Savoie wanted me to stay here for ten days and take it easy before going back to Sugluk, so I should be returning on Wednesday, weather permitting, of course. I am looking forward to getting 'home' again and back to work. There will be a lot of catching up to do after two months away.

Connie and Alice seem to be enjoying it here but find the Indians more difficult to work with than the Eskimos.

On Monday Susie came out on escort with a sick baby from Sugluk. Father Verspeek has been very busy she told me and there are a lot of chickenpox cases.

CHAPTER 8
SUGLUK 1970 (continued)

July 28th 1970
SUGLUK

I am now finally back in Sugluk! The plane had been due to leave on Wednesday the 15th but it was stranded in POV with bad weather. It eventually got back to Great Whale on the Friday but as there were so many passengers and so much cargo for POV and Harrison they couldn't take anyone or anything to Sugluk. The plane was loaded and while still on the runway, the pilot learned that the weather north was 'zero, zero'. After taxiing for about twenty minutes apparently a tourist commented what a smooth flight it was! On Saturday they finally made it and the plane returned to Great Whale the following morning. Madonne, Lorenzo and the children were also waiting to go to Sugluk after a holiday and we finally left at 12.30 on the Sunday.

It is good to be back again especially as I originally only left for three days. It has taken me a while to get used to there being no snow. At first it seemed really strange every time I looked out of the window and kept expecting to have to walk up six steps in the ice when I came out of the house. All the teachers are out on holiday and a lot of Eskimos have moved into tents. There is a row of tents down by the water and one or two families have gone out to an island for the summer.

I started work with a vengeance as soon as I got back. I was called at midnight for a sick baby and got to bed at 1 a.m. I was woken at 8 a.m. for a woman in labour who delivered a nine pound, two ounce baby girl at 2 p.m. so I kept her for the night. I was glad to go home to the trailer the next day. I also had a lot of paperwork to do with four patients going out on that Wednesday.

Last Wednesday's plane came on Thursday. We had been told it was overnighting in POV on Thursday night, so when we heard it circling overhead at 8 p.m. nobody was ready and I had a terrible time trying to find my patients but they all eventually turned up. A dentist was also on the plane. I went with my patients to the plane in the canoe and by the time I got back the dentist had disappeared. I eventually found him with Lorenzo.

This week I have 15 patients going out so I have been inundated with paper work. Because there are so many I have had to charter a plane. We were expecting the plane on Monday from POV but as the weather has been bad we haven't had it yet. I have instructed all the patients to stand by in case we have a repetition of last week's chaos. We have been having strong gales again but it is quite warm.

It has been pretty cramped in the clinic this week with all the dental equipment and Dr Gagnon, the dentist, seeing his patients at the same time as me seeing mine but we are managing well despite the lack of room. He is not impressed by the antique dental equipment which came up from our Montreal office!

I had a lot of post when I got back, including a new album of famous symphonies. I just about know the album of concertos off by heart having listened to them so often. Now I will have some new music to listen to. Claire has been sending me tapes she has recorded from QMFM Montreal radio so I can listen to the 'radio' on my tape recorder too.

If I hadn't pleaded with Montreal to let me go back to Great Whale early, still officially on sick leave, I would not be sitting here now. The Sunday plane from Toronto to Timmins, which I should have been on, blew up after take-off and everyone was killed. About twenty on board I think, including some medical personnel but no-one I knew. Quite a thought.

August 16th 1970

The ships have been coming in since July 30th and the first, the Sir Humphrey Gilbert, brought most of my sea-lift (annual supplies). It was quite a challenge ordering all my medical supplies for a year! This ship also brought the two new trailers for the new nursing station. I was so excited and wanted to see inside them straightaway. Unfortunately they were locked up and M. Gervais had the keys. I would have to wait for his visit the following week. As it happened I was so busy that week that I hardly had time to think about them. As I didn't want to move all my supplies twice, I piled them up in front of the health centre while waiting for the new clinic to be set up. Because Father Verspeek had been busy doing my job while I was away, he hadn't had time to level out the ground. The Muskeg tractor had broken down and couldn't be used to fetch gravel from up in the hills, so when M. Gervais arrived on the 7th all they could do was move the trailers nearer to mine and wait. At least I have been able to see inside them now. When they are back-to-back there will be two patient rooms; bathroom and clinic in one side, waiting room, X-ray and dark room and storage space in the other. I was hoping to set it all up before I leave here before the freeze-up but I doubt if it will be ready by then. It's very disappointing. It would have been a job after my own heart.

That Thursday (30th) I was called at 8 p.m. for Elisapee having a secondary post-partum haemorrhage. Another midwife's nightmare. I had delivered her nine days previously. I had to rush her up to the health centre; Father Verspeek kindly fetched her with his jeep. I set up an intravenous drip and went to radio Montreal about arranging a charter for the next day. I stayed up all night with Elisapee and by the morning she had stopped bleeding. I couldn't escort her myself because I still had the dentist here. As Elisapee's condition was stable by then, Father Verspeek went as escort. He hadn't been out of Sugluk for four years so he was quite excited about his trip to Frobisher Bay, returning via Montreal. There had been a Canso in POV but the pilot, for some reason, refused to come out. This is quite a scandal as medical emergencies have priority over everything. I don't know who the pilot was but I know Steve would have been here straightaway. I had to inform Dr Savoie who will investigate the matter. In the meantime there was a Beech coming in from Wakeham Bay so it was eventually 3.30 before Elisapee got away. She apparently haemorrhaged again at the hospital but at least she was in the right place. She will be OK.

On the Wednesday Dr Gagnon was expecting to fly out and despite my telling him we would be unlikely to have a plane, he couldn't believe it. He was desperate to go home. I don't think he was very happy here.

On the Sunday the Maclean ship was in and some of us were invited on board for a chat and a drink. Dr Gagnon had extracted a tooth for their helicopter pilot so he and I were fetched by helicopter!

That week we also had the first white (the bride dressed in white) wedding ever in Sugluk: Alacie and Kakinik, a very nice young couple. They had one bridesmaid. At the end of the service, which lasted about an hour, the couple stood in the porch and shook hands with everyone as they came out. Unfortunately it was raining which was a shame for them. I don't know if there was a reception. This was also the first Eskimo wedding I had seen.

The following Thursday evening, a week after Elisapee's emergency, I had another. Susie called me to say that Kautsak was in labour. I had wanted Kautsak to go to hospital for this baby as she had a very bad obstetric history and this was her tenth pregnancy but she had refused to go. When I explained the seriousness of it she said if she was going to die, she wanted to die in Sugluk. Her husband was extremely worried and could not persuade her to go to hospital either. So now she was in labour. I went round to her house and she was installed on a mattress on the floor. At 6 p.m. she delivered a lovely baby boy with no problem whatsoever. It was too good to be true. No sign of the placenta though and a few minutes later Kautsak went into shock. I called Rona who collected some things from the health centre and we managed to put up a drip, which unfortunately didn't last long as Kautsak's veins were collapsed by now. She drifted in and out of consciousness but there was nothing we could do. I sat with her and the family until 2 a.m. The family sat around drinking tea, eating bannock and fish and had a huge jig-saw out on the floor. As Kautsak's condition was fairly stable by then I went to the health centre for a couple of hours' sleep before starting to write up her papers. There was a Beech in so I went to find the pilot who agreed to take Kautsak to Frobisher Bay. At 5.30 a.m. I called Dr Savoie to let her know. As luck would have it, the weather was 'out' in Frobisher but it was good in Chimo. I decided that as there was at least a doctor in Chimo, it was best she should go there rather than stay here. I couldn't escort her as I was expecting a delegation from Ottawa that day and Father Verspeek was not yet back from escorting Elisapee. So I sent Susie, who is thoroughly reliable and very intelligent. Luckily I had a second stretcher and we organised some men to take Kautsak out to a canoe for the plane.

Susie would have liked to be a nurse but she lacked the educational qualifications, having spent several years as a child in a TB sanatorium. A great pity as she has a lot of potential. I have taught her many things and she learns quickly. She often anticipates what I am going to need for basic treatments and will have equipment ready for me. Her English of course is excellent and she has a lovely personality. I would certainly recommend her if it were possible.

The Beech left with Susie and Kautsak at 8 a.m. I came back to the health centre to run my clinic without an interpreter. By now I can manage most of the basics anyway so it wasn't a problem. It was a busy clinic. About an hour later, imagine my dismay, to see the Beech returning. I thought the weather must have deteriorated but Kautsak's family, as well as the rest of the population, thought Kautsak must have died in the plane. As it happened, it was a different Beech and we all breathed a sigh of relief.

At 12 o'clock the delegation from Ottawa arrived: Mlle Laurin, two doctors and a representative from the Canadian Nursing Association. They were visiting places in the North West Territories and the Eastern Arctic to discuss various nursing problems. We had intensive discussions all afternoon until 4 p.m. when they had to move on to Cape Dorset and Frobisher Bay. It had been very stimulating and I was sorry to see them go. Dr Gagnon was still stranded here so he took off with them.

I have been fishing nearly every day but haven't been lucky this year. I caught one but lost it. I have however been given some char. They are much bigger here than in George River where they were about two to three pounds, here, they are around eight pounds. Apparently it is not a good year. Of course, nowhere could be better than George River for fishing! It is difficult to believe that a year ago I was still there, so much has happened since.

I have developed an interest in Arctic flowers and am collecting them, pressing them in scrap books. Vera lent me an illustrated flora of the Canadian Arctic. There are 340 species available in the Arctic, of which 100 to 200 can be found in Sugluk. The book is in black and white so it is not easy identifying them. There are four pages just on different grasses. I have 50 species from Sugluk, 20 from George River and a few from Great Whale but I haven't even identified half of them yet.

I spent last week testing schoolchildren's vision, in preparation for the two ophthalmologists who are arriving tomorrow for four days. I also have a list of adults who want to see them.

This Thursday I half expected another emergency but my night's sleep was uninterrupted. Dr Savoie was also coming in for her annual visit. If it was fine the plan was to pick me up and go into Ivujivik for a couple of hours but the weather here was 'zero zero' so they wouldn't even leave POV. The weather cleared a bit later and I prepared supper for six after hearing they might come after all. We heard the plane circling overhead about 7 p.m. The water was so rough we didn't think they would make it but they did. So Dr Savoie, Ora, Dr Pellerin (the new area director), Dr Aubin from Ottawa and Mona, a new nurse who will be working in Great Whale, all came in. It was fun having everyone here but they had to leave on Sunday morning, except Mona who is staying here for a week so that I can give her some orientation before she goes to Great Whale. They also thought I could do with some help. She seems to be enjoying it here anyway.

The Hudson's Bay ship also came in last week and that was the busiest unloading of all. All the Eskimos helped to carry the boxes up to the Bay. They could only work on the high tide as the water is too shallow at low tide. High tide was between 5 a.m. and 6 a.m. and 11 hours later so it has been very hectic for Terry. The Bay is just about drained of all supplies now and it will be awhile before the new stock is put out.

I think I must hold the record for evacuations to hospital this year! I had 17 one week. I used to get everyone to the health centre half an hour before the plane was due but these days, it is rare that the plane arrives on the right day, let alone the right time so now I'm telling all the patients to go down to the beach as soon as they hear the plane and I will meet them down there with all their papers.

As I have decided to go home for Christmas and take some time off back in Europe for a few months before deciding what to do next, it means I will have to leave Sugluk before the freeze-up. I shall be going to POV for a month but don't yet know where they will send me after that. The new nurse for Sugluk will be coming at the beginning of September and I shall spend a couple of weeks with her to show her the ropes before I leave here.

September 7th 1970 Monday

We have had our first frost and all the flowers have disappeared so I'm glad I started collecting when I did. I have over 100 specimens now but still need to identify most of them.

The ophthalmologists were supposed to come in on Wednesday 19th (Aug.) and charter out again on Sunday 23rd but the plane only made it here on the Saturday so they had to change their plans. They still wanted to leave after four days, which would be the Tuesday (25th) so we started work straightaway, worked all day on the Sunday and finished on the Monday so they were ready to leave on the Tuesday. Needless to say, there was no plane that Tuesday! However, unlike Dr Gagnon, who had been so anxious to get away, these ophthalmologists really enjoyed their little holiday. It was good fun having them here and they had come stocked up with wine. They wanted to try all the local produce so we had char and polar bear meat amongst other things. They finally got away on the Friday. Mona also left on that plane. She had enjoyed herself here and was a great help to me.

Since then I have been trying to tidy up and prepare for the new nurse, who should have been here last Wednesday but we haven't had a plane since the others left. We had a fantastic storm one night, with gale-force winds all night. The noise with my trailer and the two new ones parked close by was incredible. It was impossible to sleep.

Last week a plane came in from Ivujivik with three sick children on board. Steve, the Ivujivik lay dispenser, is on holiday at the moment so the pilot notified me that all three children had pneumonia. I went down to meet the plane wondering what to expect. Eighteen-month-old Adamie and his three-year-old sister and another four-year-old were brought out. Adamie was barely conscious and GREY! I was horrified. I ran with him in my arms all the way to the health centre and crammed him into the incubator and turned on the oxygen while I prepared the oxygen tent. I really didn't want to lose another baby. I nursed him all day and night and thankfully he recovered enough to go home. The other two children were not as ill as Adamie and were able to be looked after by Eskimo families.

The Canada Geese have started flying south so that is a sign that winter is on the way. Sometimes there are really big flocks and it is fascinating watching them fly in formation. They can be heard quite a way off so I have had enough time to get my camera.

We had a charter in yesterday, (Sunday) with three new teachers. They are a bit lost at the moment as Mike and Elizabeth are stuck in Great Whale. School is supposed to start again on Wednesday so I hope they are back by then.

I am trying to pack for POV and am still waiting for my replacement.

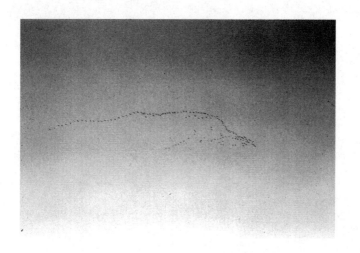

Canada Geese flying south (NB formation)

CHAPTER 9
POVUNGNITUK AND GREAT WHALE
RIVER 1970

September 23rd 1970
POVUNGNITUK

My last week in Sugluk was pretty hectic. I sent out most of my boxes on the plane to POV in advance and Andrée, the new nurse, finally arrived on that plane. I showed her around, introduced her to everyone and initiated her as best I could in just a week. I think she will enjoy Sugluk. I was very sad to leave after such an amazing year and having gained so much experience but I do feel in need of a holiday now. On September 13th we woke up to find the mountains covered in snow. The first snow of a new season.

The day after I sent out my luggage to POV, I radioed the nurses just to check they had received it. They hadn't. One of them went to investigate and found my box still on the beach having been drowned by the high tide! They kindly unpacked it and dried out as much as they could for me. My violin was in the box so I was anxious to see what damage had been done. All my slides were also there but as I had packed them in plastic boxes inside plastic bags as an extra precaution it seemed they were OK. And they are, much to my relief. The violin will need some re-glueing.

I was ready to leave last Wednesday but as usual, there was no plane. It was delayed for several days, finally arriving on Sunday! (September 20th). For some reason we headed north and circled over Raglan Lake. For a while I thought we were going to spend the night on the lake but we finally arrived in POV three hours later. There was no-one to meet me so I made my way to the nursing station where I found Louise in the midst of a medical emergency. She was getting the patient ready to leave on that plane and escort her herself. Lise was not there either so I was left on my own for the night until Louise returned the following day. The Monday morning clinic was pretty busy but not complicated so I just got on with it. The plane did not return as planned so I spent the evening with Father Steinmann, the Catholic missionary. He had been to see me earlier and invited me over. He is a great character, good fun and very dynamic. He is French and has been up here for 13 years. He too, like Father Verspeek has had his share of lay-dispensing and acts as the dentist. I took the clinic again on Tuesday morning and sadly, later, received a telegram to say that Louise's patient had died in hospital so I had to go and break the news to the family which was rather harrowing. Louise eventually came back that evening, to my relief.

October 1st 1970

I was supposed to stay in POV for a month but on Thursday 24th (after only four days) we had a message to say there was a place in a permanent institution for little Bobby who is five and a half, mentally and physically handicapped and unable to walk, so he obviously needed an escort and it made sense for me to go with him. I had to pack up all my belongings again and take them to Great Whale as I would not be coming back to POV. The plane left at 8 a.m. the next day. Bobby was very good but needs constant attention. We found a family in Great Whale where Bobby could stay for the weekend, awaiting our flight south. It is amazing how one can always find families willing to look after patients from other settlements, however ill or handicapped. The Eskimos are so hospitable.

Mona has now gone to POV, Connie was stuck in the Belcher Islands so Alice was glad of my help with her Friday clinic. As the weather was bad in the Belcher Islands, Connie was still stranded on the Monday. I helped Alice with her clinic and on Tuesday I went to fetch Bobby and we boarded the Nordair jet at 11.30 a.m.

We arrived in Montreal two hours later but no-one was there to meet us. I phoned the office and as they had been unable to contact Great Whale, they didn't know when we would be arriving so hadn't arranged an escort for Bobby. I offered to take him myself so they sent a car for us. Bobby was very restless by now so it wasn't an easy ride. The hospital for severely mentally and physically handicapped children is in Drummondsville, about 65 miles from Montreal. The staff were very interested to know about the Eskimo lifestyle and the sort of life Bobby had. They showed me round the hospital which I found very depressing as all the children are the worst cases and will never be able to function at home. The driver took me back to Montreal and just ten minutes from Montreal he hit another car! Nothing serious but we had to wait for the police to come and papers were exchanged. I finally got to Claire's at 6.30 p.m. It was good to see her again, we had a lot of catching up to do as usual.

Yesterday I spent most of the day in the office. I have also booked my flight home for Christmas. I was lucky to get a flight as most of them are fully booked already from the 19th December. I have a seat for December 20th arriving at London airport at 10 a.m. on the 21st. I'm very excited about going home. I shall have spent almost two years in the Arctic by then.

October 22nd 1970
GREAT WHALE RIVER

Connie and Alice are now both in Great Whale. Last week we had an emergency from POV. Mona was not able to tell us much except that she was escorting out an unconscious patient. We went to meet the plane to find that her patient was our colleague Louise, who had had some sort of cerebral episode. We were all very worried and Mona was exhausted. They were taken straight to Montreal by DC4. Louise is apparently fine now but will not be returning. Pam, who was in POV some years ago is going back to POV so she and Mona will be based there.

I am doing the school nursing now in Great Whale which is busy as there are about 225 schoolchildren. They all need their annual fluoride toothpaste treatments and immunisations. The Eskimo children seem brighter than the Indians but that is mainly because the Eskimos are no longer nomadic and the Cree still spend winters in the bush so don't have as much schooling. At least they are not forgetting their traditions.

October 27th 1970

It is good fun here in Great Whale, with the three of us. The boys from the DOT often come over. We have good parties at the weekends and plenty of late nights. The Northern Lights (Aurora Borealis) are fantastic here. I have never seen them like this before. I am trying to capture them on my camera but it is not easy as they move quite fast. So far I have only seen them green and yellow but they can be other colours too. Pan Am has a permanent research station here studying the Aurora so I must go down sometime and see it. Another phenomenon here is noctilucent clouds - some sort of phosphorescent effect apparently. October is the last month they can be seen so I may not be lucky. Sunset is now at 4.30 p.m. Just three months ago it was at 10.30! We have had a little snow here but it has melted again.

I am still busy with the schoolchildren but have run out of fluoride toothpaste so I'll have to start the immunisations while I am waiting for new supplies.

November 15th 1970

Time is flying by, less than three weeks before I leave here. I have just about finished all the immunisations now and am going to start some health teaching this week.

The first permanent snow came a week ago so all the ski-doos are out again. Peter, Paul and Pierre are around here a lot and we have been out ski-dooing most evenings this week. We often go down to the bar for parties as well as having them here.

On Saturday morning I went down to North Camp, a couple of miles from here, where the research stations are. Paul works with magnetic fields, studying earthquakes etc. There are permanent graphs registering and photographing the earth's movements and Paul has to change the films and check machinery every 24 hours. I was a bit out of my depth but it was interesting. Peter works for Pan Am and he showed me his station studying the Aurora Borealis. He also has permanent graphs and a camera constantly photographing the sky and has to check the equipment every 24 hours and change the film. Unfortunately he has to send the films south so he doesn't see the results. Apparently the Aurora phenomenon is still a complete mystery.

December 2nd 1970

It has been a hectic three weeks. The house has been painted and we have been living with the smell of paint. We kept having to move from one room to another, move the clinic upstairs and back again. Connie and I spent three nights in the trailer which is for transient quarters, (visiting doctors, dentists etc.) We spent another three nights in the cold storage room in the basement. We were finally back in our own rooms and a couple of days later a hot water pipe burst in the basement. There were several inches of steaming water down there and we spent the afternoon baling out and clearing up. Then, that same week we had salt in the water for three days because of exceptionally high tides which spread to the river. We had to melt snow for making coffee.

We had a visit from Mlle Laurin who spent a couple of days here before visiting the other places. Ora is on a course in Ottawa this year. That weekend was my last weekend here and we hoped we would be able to have a party with the boys. It wasn't sure with Mlle Laurin's visit. Unbeknown to me, the others were trying to organise a surprise birthday party for me and on the Saturday morning they tried unsuccessfully to get me out on my ski-doo. It wasn't a very nice day and I just wanted to laze around at home. In the afternoon Alice persuaded me to go to the co-op with her. When we got back Connie suddenly became very keen to do some French (I have been teaching her). I was amazed but of course couldn't pass up such an opportunity. She suggested we go to the trailer for our lesson so this we did. I was delighted with her enthusiasm, I must say! We came back for supper and to my surprise the tables were set, guests had arrived and there was a pile of presents! I was quite overcome as my birthday wasn't till the next day but as Pierre had to work on Sunday they decided to celebrate it on the Saturday. I understood later how uncooperative I had been all day! Connie had had to ice the cake in the X-ray room in case I suddenly appeared. Earlier that week Maggie, an Eskimo who makes exquisite dolls, had arrived with the dolls Connie and Alice had ordered for me and was in the clinic when I came home early from school. The others were in the middle of paying for the dolls when they heard me come in. They hid Maggie in a corner with her hood up, Alice stood with the dolls behind her and Elisapi, the interpreter daren't say a word to Maggie in case I understood. Connie rushed me upstairs to have an urgent consultation on what to have for lunch (it was apparently 11 a.m.). I don't remember the day at all! Maggie was a good sport, she knew what was going on. On the Sunday, which was my birthday, we had a special breakfast with pancakes and strawberries. What a fantastic birthday! So now, I'm 31.

We have had storms for a week, there has been a lot of snow and there are deep drifts everywhere. Connie has been on the Belcher Islands and unable to get back here. I have stayed on an extra week while she was there but she may not get back before I leave now. Temperatures are in the 20s here and apparently Churchill, the other side of the Hudson Bay, have already had 30 below zero. I am leaving here on Tuesday 8th and am spending 12 days in Montreal before leaving for London. Not long now!

Mlle Laurin has been trying to persuade me to go to university to do the Public Health Nursing Diploma. The government would sponsor me and I could choose which university I would like. She says Vancouver offers a good course. She understands that I want to spend a few months back home in Europe and has offered me six months extended leave to think about it. The course lasts one academic year (nine months) and I would have to give back 18 months in the Arctic, in return. I must let her know before June 1971 if I want to start that September. She tried to persuade me last year but I said I wasn't interested in public health. All I can remember about lectures on public health as a student nurse, are how many gallons of water it takes to flush a toilet, that a window must be a minimum of a tenth of the floor space and that we visited a sewage farm on a foggy day in London in 1959. This year, I told her again I wasn't interested and whereas last year she didn't press me, this year she asked me what I thought I was doing every day in the Arctic. It had never occurred to me that this was public health nursing! So now I am thinking about it differently. Anyway I have six months to consider it.

Apart from wanting to go home and see everyone, I also want to visit all my friends on the continent. The other big reason is to see Geoffrey again and see whether we are going to get married. It was unfortunate that we only met a few weeks before I was leaving for Canada but it was 'love at first sight', for
me anyway. Although we have been writing to each other it is difficult to know for sure. We have not discussed marriage and I might feel differently when I see him again. At least I shall have time to see everyone.

PART TWO 1971

I had a wonderful six months in Europe and managed to visit all my friends in England, France, Spain, Denmark and Germany. Geoffrey and I met up several times which was good but I don't think either of us was ready to marry. We will stay in touch though. I decided to return to Canada and take up the offer of a place at the University of British Columbia, Vancouver in September 1971. I returned to Canada with the Empress of Canada, which took seven days. I met Peter on the ship; he was going to work in a bank in Ontario. We were both attracted to each other and planned to meet again. I returned to Great Whale River in June where I was to fill in those three months.

CHAPTER 10
GREAT WHALE RIVER 1971

June 17th 1971
GREAT WHALE RIVER

I arrived here on June 1st and it was snowing! What a contrast with Montreal where temperatures were in the 80s. It was back to winter clothes again. This week has been warmer with temperatures in the 70s and as there are no mosquitoes yet we can walk around in short sleeves. The sunsets are lovely at the moment, around 9.30 to 10 p.m.

Connie and Alice are still here but all the DOT boys except Pierre have left so it seems very quiet without the old crowd. Connie was to have gone to Vancouver with me in September but she is getting married to Steve, who is a teacher at the federal school. Mona, who is still in POV, may take her place.

After my three months in the north I shall probably get about a week's holiday so I shall have time to take the train across Canada from Montreal to Vancouver. Another new experience for me. I think it takes about four days. It will be wonderful to see the Rockie Mountains too.

We aren't very busy here at the moment but Connie will be leaving on Tuesday so that will probably change. I may be going to Port Harrison or POV in August, it hasn't been decided yet.

June 26th 1971

We are having real 'November' weather here! We have had snow and storms and been closed-in for three days. We could soon get the ski-doo out if this continues. Ora has been here since Tuesday and is waiting for the next plane out. We have been playing tennis (indoors, of course). I hadn't played for years. There is a court at the club.

July 16th 1971

Our weather now is cold, wet and foggy. We went for 12 days without the jet after last month's snow storms.

I have started driving the jeep. It is much bigger than our little jeep in Chimo. This is more like a station wagon. It is automatic drive but very hard to get into four-wheel-drive. There is nothing but sand here so it skids quite a bit. The other night two patients came down from POV; I went to meet them with the jeep and had to find somewhere for them to stay. Zebedee, an Eskimo who is originally from POV, came with me. He is a great character and is always helping people in need. If it hadn't been for him I would never have got the jeep into four-wheel-drive and I would have had to abandon it in the sand.

We almost had a tragedy a couple of weeks ago when the Lawrences' (Anglican minister's family) two little girls, Fiona aged four and Karen two, were playing outside when Maureen called them in to lunch. Fiona came in but there was no sign of Karen. She had been playing near Caleb's motor bike when it fell on her, across her neck. Caleb found her just in time but thought she was dead as she was blue and not breathing. They called us straightaway and as there was a visiting doctor here on his way to POV we took him with us. By now Karen was breathing again but deeply unconscious. Connie escorted her out to hospital an hour later and her condition deteriorated in the plane. She had to have an emergency tracheotomy in a little outpost hospital and was then taken to Montreal. Alice and I were left trying to comfort Maureen and Caleb and none of us knew at that stage if Karen would live or die. I felt so helpless. We didn't know what to say. She is apparently doing well now and should soon be home again. Let's hope there isn't too much brain damage.

Maureen and Caleb, whom I hadn't met before, are such a nice couple, both Irish.

July 24th 1971

I went out on escort about 10 days ago with a woman from POV who had a ruptured appendix. Ora had been in POV and escorted her here. I took over the escort to Moosonee, in a Canso. All went well and a doctor came out to the plane in a canoe and took the patient to hospital so I didn't even get out of the plane. By the time I got back here I had spent six hours in the Canso. I don't like travelling in the Canso, it is the one plane that makes me feel sick with the petrol fumes.

Little Karen came back this week and has made a complete recovery. That is a miracle!

The weather isn't improving; it is still very foggy and now the mosquitoes are around again too.

My course at the University of British Columbia in Vancouver starts about September 14th but I have to be there a week beforehand to register. On August 2nd I am to go to POV for 12 days.

August 23rd 1971
MONTREAL

I spent ten days in POV with Pam who is English. I had met her briefly last year on her way back to POV for the second time. We were pretty busy the whole time and we worked very well together. She is a lovely person and we had good fun too. We had an emergency with a woman who had a suspected collapsed lung after delivery. Fortunately Pam is also a midwife. We had to get the midwifery textbook out as this is one of those obstetric emergencies rarely seen. Fortunately the patient recovered. I had a lot of nights working so had to catch up on sleep when I got back to Great Whale. Ann, a Scottish nurse has just gone up to POV for a year so it was useful that I was there while Pam was showing Ann around. While I was still in POV I had to go up to Sugluk to fetch a stretcher case. This turned out to be Mary, my first interpreter, who was having pregnancy complications. I didn't actually go into the village, Chris and Rona came out on that plane to go on holiday and told me that Father Verspeek is apparently away somewhere and Terry and Vera have moved to Cape Dorset. Mary stayed the night in the nursing station in POV and her condition remained stable. The following day I escorted her to Moosonee, which was EIGHT hours in the Canso. (!!) Mary continued to be stable and I was apparently looking sicker than my patient by the time we arrived. (I felt it too!) We were met by canoe and taken down the river to Moose Factory hospital which is on an island. It was pouring with rain and they covered us with tarpaulins for the half-hour journey. I saw Mary settled on the ward and then spent the night at the hospital myself.

The next morning the sun was shining and I enjoyed the half hour up the river in the canoe. This time I got the DC3 (thank goodness!) back to Great Whale. Dr Savoie and team arrived for their annual visit, stayed one night and left for Port Harrison at 5 p.m. the next day. At 9 p.m. to our amazement, they were back with us. Apparently when they landed in Port Harrison the water was so rough that no-one could come out to the plane to meet them so the pilot had to return to Great Whale. Later we learned that earlier in the day, a canoe had capsized near Port Harrison, with six people in it including the DOT cook who had drowned. No wonder no-one wanted to go out on the water again that day, they must have been terrified. What a terrible experience for the village.

I am now on holiday so I am going to Toronto to visit Peter, who I met on the Empress of Canada and pick up the train from there to Vancouver. I hope to see the Rockies by day.

VANCOUVER: After an exciting three days and nights on the train from Toronto to Vancouver I booked into a hotel as I would not be able to move into the students' residence for a few days. The next morning I made my way to the university. A letter from my father was waiting for me

in the students' office and I put it in my pocket to read later when I had finished registering for all the courses. Registration seemed very complicated to me and it was 4 o'clock when I got back to the hotel. My father's letter had some shocking news: my mother was in hospital in Taunton, dying of lung cancer. The letter was already ten days old so I had no idea if she was still alive or not. I sent a telegram to my father to say I was flying home the following day. (He was not on the phone). I flew home and spent ten days at home, visiting my mother every day with my father. It was a very sad time and I had to return to Vancouver to begin the course. The hardest thing for me was to say goodbye to my mother, knowing I would never see her again. She was only 56. She died a week after I returned to Vancouver.

Back in Vancouver, where I didn't know a soul, was quite hard but I soon made some friends and Betty and Gary who had two young children, invited me to their place many weekends and were very supportive. The community health nursing diploma was very stimulating and I was particularly drawn to the psychological aspects. I did some field work among Indians in Kitimat which was interesting. At the end of the course I went home for a holiday before starting work at Great Whale River.

CHAPTER 11
GREAT WHALE RIVER 1972

July 10th 1972
GREAT WHALE RIVER

I left home on June 18th after my holiday in England, to fly out on the 19th, the day of the strike. Air Canada was on strike but they had chartered Dan Air to fly to Montreal. Passengers were asked to be at Heathrow at 10.30 a.m. ready to fly at 12 p.m. I arrived at 10 o'clock and learned that Dan Air weren't allowed into Heathrow so all passengers were being taken by coach to Gatwick at 10.45. We eventually left at 11.30 for the one and a half hour journey to Gatwick. We were told that probable departure time would be about 2.30 p.m. so everyone made a bee-line for the cafeteria. I had my sandwich in my hand when we they announced we could board. Some poor people never even got their food, I was lucky. We boarded at 1.30 and then waited and waited and waited. The captain kept apologising for the delay and thanked us for our patience. Apparently we were waiting for our luggage. We finally took off at 3.15 p.m. and our midday meal was served at 5.30. I have never heard so many screaming children. We finally arrived in Montreal seven hours later. I was supposed to leave for Great Whale the following morning and prayed for bad weather to give me time to recover. My prayers were duly answered, the plane was cancelled. The following day it was cancelled again.

Great Whale is much the same as ever, we had some snow last week (July 3rd) and the weather is as temperamental as it always is in the summer. I have been back just over two weeks now. Pam is going to Montreal so that is disappointing as I was looking forward to working with her here. So it will just be Connie and me after September and I shall be in charge. Of course, now she is married, Connie will be living with Steve in a teacher's house. I shall be living on my own in the nursing station.

The village is a bit chaotic at the moment as all the Indian houses are being moved around and nobody knows where anyone lives any more. I heard about an Indian who went home for lunch one day and couldn't find his house.

We had a total eclipse of the sun today which was very exciting. Everything went dark, it was quite weird, I took some photos but have no idea how they will turn out.

July 29th 1972

I have now been back for nearly six weeks and time is flying by as it always does in the north.

John Masty is still our Cree interpreter-cum-handyman etc. He is quite a character and some of the interpreting is very long-winded. For example, the other day I asked John to ask the patient how long he had had the pain. A long conversation then followed. When I asked John what the patient said, he told me, "He said 'yes' " and we had to start again!

We had a team of film-makers up here, making a video tape for National Health and Welfare. The aim of it is to be able to show prospective nurses intending to work in the Arctic, what life is like up here. They have spent a good deal of time filming us at work and having interviews with us.

I had to sit up all night one night with a young French Canadian woman who was suicidal. Her husband had just dragged her out of the river. Poor man, he was naturally very distressed. He escorted her out the next day and she is now in hospital. The Arctic is not the ideal place for depression. A French Canadian man, in his 50s, in charge of the provincial government garage came to see me one day, asking for tranquillisers. He was in tears, when he told me that he had been led to believe he would be in charge of a big modern garage and showroom, only to find he was repairing ski-doos in a draughty old hangar. He had left his wife in Quebec and hoped to make a lot of money for their retirement. He was miserable, homesick and very disillusioned. (How I felt for him!) I told him that being in the Arctic was not going to solve his problem and after discussion he decided to go home. I gave him some Valium to tide him over the next few days and he flew home the following week. What a sad story.

The planes are as erratic as ever. We had one arrive at 1.30 a.m. one morning, and not only that, we had to find homes for patients in transit.

I have also done my first breech delivery this week. I wasn't sure what I was feeling when I examined the woman in labour and a little foot appeared! It all went well though. Of course I don't know all the antenatal patients yet so I shall no doubt have more a few more surprises.

August 19th 1972

The ships have started coming in now. The Hudson's Bay Company ship is here; the co-op has had one but we are still waiting for our sea lift. There are all sorts of different little vehicles appearing and I have seen several little tractors running around. They will probably be good on snow too.

I had a telegram from Montreal asking me to apply for the position of Zone Nursing Officer (this zone). I have mixed feelings about it though; promotion would be good but I'm not sure I would survive the office in Montreal. Anyway I can always turn it down if I do get it. I think I'm going to enjoy Great Whale. It's a funny place but it is very challenging with its mix of people and the demands of a bigger settlement.

I have had some busy nights what with a delivery and an unexpected death which was rather a shock; I had a phone call from David Stone (Eskimo) in the middle of the night and he simply said, "Louisa Stone is dead!" I went straight over to his house. He had woken and found his wife lying dead beside him. Although she had chronic emphysema, her death was unexpected. I stayed with David for awhile and gave him what comfort I could, it was very sad.

The other day an Eskimo man came to ask me to remove a piece of metal which had become embedded in his thigh when it shot out of the stove. I said I wasn't really supposed to do things like that but he was so desperate, I said I would try but couldn't promise success. I injected local anaesthetic and proceeded to dig with a scalpel. After about 20 minutes, I still hadn't found the metal when someone knocked at the door. The moment I looked up, I suddenly felt the metal under the scalpel! I got it out, stitched the skin up and sent home a very happy, satisfied patient.

We have had a lot of fog here this year but Sugluk has had a terrible summer. There is still ice floating around on the bay apparently and they have hardly had any planes. And it's almost time for the freeze-up!

September 1st 1972

Last Sunday Caleb and Maureen Lawrence's new baby Sean was christened. He is nine months old. They had been waiting for the bishop of the Arctic to come. Many of the significant people were absent, including Maureen who had suddenly had to go to hospital so I was asked to stand in for her. The Godparents were also 'proxy'. The church was packed with Eskimos and Indians and the service was taken in the three languages.

The other night I noticed a very strong smell of petrol coming through the windows at the back of the house. We keep our drums at the back and I was afraid one of the Indians who is a known 'gas-sniffer' was out there. I was afraid to go out there on my own so phoned Bob the administrator and he came round straightaway. We went out with a torch and examined the drums which were all intact. No sign of unconscious Indians. Suddenly Bob realised what it was - the Shell oil tanker was on the bay for the annual replenishment and the wind was blowing off the sea! We had a good laugh.

I have several potted plants here and I get quite excited when a new leaf appears. Anything green in the Arctic is to be treasured. I was looking after some of the teachers' plants while they were on holiday and one of the teachers has given me two of his.

September 18th 1972

Great Whale is calming down a bit after the summer which always brings an influx of transient visitors. Now all the teachers and 'permanent' people are back again. I think it promises to be a good year. Connie and Steve came to my place for supper on Saturday. I did a baked ham with the American glazing of Molasses and mustard. At the weekends I have more time to experiment with cooking. We then went down to the club for a party. We have got one or two good musicians and have a nice band. Chuck, who works at the Bay, is a fantastic drummer. We were dancing until 2 a.m.

On Friday I had a little trip to Fort George with a very sick baby with gastroenteritis. He arrived on the plane from Port Harrison the day before and I was up all night with him. His condition deteriorated during the night so I chartered the Canso which was already here, the next morning. I didn't go into the village when we got to Fort George, we just stopped long enough for me to hand over the baby. I had my first flying lesson on the way back! The pilot let me take the controls and I learned how to keep it in a straight line, go up or down and over sideways. Naturally I had to go back to my seat for the landing. We had our first snow that day too (September 14th).

All our sea lift has come in now so we have been busy unpacking it.

I went to supper with Maureen and Caleb last Tuesday and watched some of their slides of Great Whale several years ago. All their children are fine. We still can't believe the miracle of little Karen. Maureen is a professional cook and has given me a wonderful recipe for Christmas pudding. I have made my first batch already.

Yesterday I had supper with Jean and Peter Arthur, both teachers from Trinidad. They have just started their third year here and I met them last year. They had never seen snow before they came up here, it was an amazing experience for them.

There were some beautiful Northern Lights here last week and I did some experimenting photographing them, with the camera on the tripod, varying the shutter speed. I am keeping records of each one.

October 5th 1972

Last Monday we started the week with a plane crash! At lunch-time the Canso had just taken off from here, heading north, when after about 10 miles, one of the engines caught fire. The pilot turned back and quite a few people saw the plane with smoke coming out of it, suddenly come down and disappear behind the trees the other side of the river. Eskimos and Indians set off at once in canoes. Connie and I waited at the nursing station, not knowing what to expect. It was very nerve-wracking. (It was also baby clinic day). There were 16 people on board. Shortly afterwards a DC3 flew over the area and the pilot reported eight people walking around so we knew that at least half had survived. Not long after that, all 16 people were brought to the nursing station. They all walked through the door and most had only minor injuries but were very shocked of course. The pilot had head injuries and probably fractured ribs. Connie escorted him to hospital.

That evening a plane came from the north and I had to meet three patients and find somewhere for them to stay. I noticed one was a young 14-year-old girl (Mary) who was mentally handicapped but she was taken in by an Eskimo family. A couple of hours later I had a phone call from the family saying they couldn't cope with Mary, she was tearing the place apart. I went down to investigate, gave Mary a sedative and found another family to take her. At 11.30 p.m. they phoned to say they were having problems too so I had to fetch her here with me. She carried on being restless, throwing things around and shouting, amongst other things "Annie akualuk!" ("Big, fat, ugly Annie!") I decided to sleep in the other bed in the patient room to keep an eye on her. She continued to be disruptive and eventually I got her to sleep when I took her into my bed. She had probably never slept on her own before. As the plane didn't leave for Moose Factory until the Thursday, I had to look after Mary for three days and nights! I took her for long walks to wear her out, (unsuccessfully). As I couldn't leave her for five minutes, poor Connie had to do the clinics on her own. I didn't get much sleep those few nights. Eventually, I sent for her mother from Port Harrison to escort her to hospital. Apparently her mother can manage her. I spent the weekend recovering.

On Tuesday Mary Masty (John's wife) arrived in labour. As she was very large I had already sent her out to hospital a month previously as I thought she might have twins. She had been sent back, no twins seen and another month to go. She had been in labour for several hours and as it was her third baby, I would have expected her to have delivered by now. I was very worried as I couldn't tell which way the baby was lying as Mary was so big and I was afraid she might obstruct in labour. If it wasn't twins, it was obviously a very big baby. As the Nordair jet was in, I decided to escort her to Montreal myself. I radioed Montreal to let them know and asked to be met with an ambulance. We left at 3.30 p.m. with Mary on a stretcher. I took a delivery pack with me. Luckily the plane was almost empty with two or three Eskimos sitting at the back. (No curious tourists wanting to know everything). There were two very young air hostesses who knew what was happening and they offered to be of any help they could. Mary was on her stretcher, fixed across two seats near the front of the plane. An hour later, halfway between Great Whale and Montreal, she delivered a big baby boy. The delivery went beautifully and the placenta also came with no problems. It was the first delivery the two air hostesses had ever seen and they were thrilled. I was also happy for them as I believe that the first delivery a woman sees or experiences is going to influence her for life. Also, air hostesses are supposed to know what to do if a woman goes into labour on a plane, so they had an excellent demonstration of a normal delivery. I just had time to clear up everything before we landed at 5.30 p.m. The ambulance was there to meet us and we were rushed to Montreal General

Hospital where it only remained to examine the placenta and weigh the baby. The nurses could not believe that Mary didn't need stitching after delivering this 10 POUND 15 OUNCE (4.96kg) baby! In retrospect, I needn't have taken Mary on a plane but this is an example of the responsibility we have. If she had obstructed in labour she could have died, so I had to make the decision, being aware of the fact that this trip would cost the government $300. If I had waited until it was a real emergency and had to charter a plane, it would have cost even more. Montreal are always very supportive though and they back up every decision we make.

I didn't know whether the baby should be registered in Great Whale or Montreal as he was born exactly halfway between the two places. I learned that a baby born in a plane has to be registered at the place of arrival so this little Cree baby will be registered in Montreal! I stayed a couple of nights with Pam, who is now living near the airport, before returning to Great Whale.

My first Aurora Borealis slides are back and out of 13, one is good and three are fair so I shall know what adjustments to make next time.

The crashed Canso is now a write-off. I learned that it was the one I had my first 'flying lesson' in! I don't think there are many Cansos left now.

October 25th 1972

The pilot from the crash has apparently made a good recovery but he has left Austin Airways and has gone out to British Columbia, I believe.

The snow is now here to stay and my ski-doo is in the garage being fixed for the winter.

There is a video player here in the nursing station and we are being sent video tapes from Montreal. I was sent a two hour film 'A Funny Thing Happened to Me on the Way to the Forum' which was really funny. I invited people round to watch. It is like having television. Actually, there is talk of getting television up here in the next year. I don't know what sort of effect that will have on life here.

As part of my programme I have just taken on the high school (secondary). There are 16 Eskimo students who come from various settlements and are residential here. I am looking forward to doing some health teaching with them, it is a nice age group to work with.

I have had quite a few visitors, nurses on their way through with patients etc. Céline was here from POV a couple of days, Denise from Port Harrison was on her way to a conference. It was the first time we had met. She will be back in a couple of weeks. It's freeze-up time now up north so we soon shan't be getting so many planes through here. (Or difficult patients!)

The social club is being rebuilt and decorated so there are no films (or bar) this week. We had a 'last' party on Thursday and danced until 1 a.m.

November 18th 1972

A couple of weeks ago I had to charter a plane for a little 11-year-old girl who had head injuries after a ski-doo accident. We flew to Fort George which is an hour south of here. I was to return the following day but the weather was bad so I had two days in Fort George. I met Ursula who is an English nurse just doing public health nursing among the Cree Indians in Fort George. She spent a year in Great Whale in 1968 and before that, a year on the Queen Charlotte Islands. After Great Whale she went back to England, then came back here and married Guy, a French Canadian teacher. We got on very well together and have a lot in common. It was good fun chatting. She told me a very amusing story: after her two year break back in England, on her way up here, she arrived at Timmins airstrip and saw two DC3s. She approached the first and found a smartly dressed air hostess waiting at the top of the steps. There were plush carpets and magazines were all but being distributed. Ursula was obviously dressed for the north and the hostess asked her where she was going. When Ursula told her, she pointed to the other plane.

Ursula found that nothing had changed, the same shabby plane, boxes of cargo everywhere and seats piled up against the toilet door. No air hostess! They took off ten minutes later, circled round a couple of times and landed again in Timmins. They had forgotten one of the co-pilots! She wondered how she could ever have mistaken Austin Airways.

We are now having some nice ski-doo outings. The weather is colder and not so damp, with daytime temperatures around 20 to 30 so the snow is perfect. It is gorgeous country around here. We need to take advantage of it now as in January and February it is too cold for ski-doo outings. Temperatures have already been down to about 20 below at night. The furnace in the trailer broke down and everything froze. I discovered it last Saturday. Water was spurting out of one of the pipes as a result of a thaw. What a mess! The plumber will have to come in and change the pipes.

Clocks went back a couple of weeks ago. Now it gets dark about 4.30 p.m. and light about 7.30 a.m.

A satellite has just been launched from Cape Kennedy for T.V and telephone for the Arctic. That will make a big change in the life up here. Once the aerials are up we will get T.V direct from the satellite.

The social club is still not finished and people are getting rather bored with nowhere to go. The last of the furnishings are supposed to be coming with Nordair.

The new prefabricated Indian houses are almost finished now. They are apparently getting plumbing too.

December 4th 1972

I had a nice birthday on November 22nd; Connie and Steve invited me for a meal that evening and gave me a miniature pair of Indian snow shoes.

It has been chaos here today! There was no electricity in the whole settlement until the afternoon. Apparently whoever was on night duty last night fell asleep and the generator packed up. Everyone was without heat or light. As the temperature is regularly down to 20 below zero at night it can be pretty cold. School was cancelled and we had to cancel our X-rays. We did our morning clinic by candlelight as there isn't much daylight in the clinic, which is in the basement.

An English nurse is missing after a Beechcraft came down somewhere in the Arctic. I believe she works in Cambridge Bay. It doesn't sound too hopeful.

Winnie, our housekeeper, has had to go to a sanatorium as she has TB, so as all of us working in the nursing station are contacts, we have had to have chest X-rays, skin tests and send out sputum specimens to Montreal.

I have decided to go to Vancouver for Christmas and stay with Betty and Gary. It will be wonderful to see them again. I will stay until January 1st.

December 23rd 1972
VANCOUVER

Our winter in Great Whale has been so severe that some of the white people had to be sent to Montreal after their houses froze up.

I managed to come out on escort as far as Montreal so that was good timing before my holiday. A young boy with some sort of schizophrenic episode needed an escort to Montreal. I took him all the way to hospital and it was 8.30 p.m. by the time I got to Pam's. (Claire and John have moved to Toronto). Pam lives close to the airport.

I am very lucky to be in Vancouver as so many of the Canadian airports have been closed-in weatherwise. Pam's neighbours drove me to the airport yesterday. It was impossible to find a taxi because they were so busy. I was supposed to fly to Vancouver from Toronto but Toronto airport had been closed-in for three days. Then I learned that my flight was cancelled and I found myself in a thronging mass of people queuing to get on another flight to Toronto. I wasn't too keen on waiting two days when Toronto wasn't even my destination. I decided to see if I could go 'stand-by' on a direct flight to Vancouver instead. It was now 5.50 p.m. and I went over to the Vancouver departure gate. There were two flights to Vancouver, one at 6.20 p.m. via Edmonton and the other at 10.30 p.m. I hoped I might get on the 10.30 or the first one the next morning if I waited around. I told the man I would like to go 'stand-by', he looked at my ticket, asked me where I would like to sit and told me boarding was in 10 minutes! I couldn't believe my luck to be on that first flight. The plane was actually half empty because of the lack of Toronto passengers but when we landed in Edmonton it completely filled up and left 140 people behind. Gary came to meet me at the airport and it is lovely to see them all again. The new baby Johanna is just six weeks old.

It is strange to see no snow, in fact it has been raining. It was 30 below when I left Great Whale but it felt much colder in Montreal with the damp even though it was only 10 below.

January 10th 1973
GREAT WHALE RIVER

I had a marvellous holiday in Vancouver and was kept very busy going to parties and visiting friends etc.. I also went over to Victoria for three days.

I left Vancouver on January 3rd and was to leave for Great Whale on the 4th but, true to form, the plane was delayed for two days. I spent a night at the Airport Inn and found others who had been waiting for six days. When it finally left, the plane was full, with 58 passengers. Quite a load.

Monday was hard getting back to work. I was up all night on Tuesday with a woman in labour who delivered just before midnight.

Everyone is still having problems with heating. I still haven't any hot water so I go over to Connie's from time to time for a bath. School is cancelled until their heating is sorted out too. The teachers are having a prolonged holiday down south as the heating in their residence is still frozen. The reason for the heating problems here is that most of the white people's houses up this end are on a communal steam central heating system and if one house has problems it means digging up half the street. Obviously with the severe temperatures, water has frozen. We have mains water here, unlike in Sugluk where each house had its individual supply. Great Whale is just on the borderline of permafrost so they can have underground pipes here but with the Arctic temperatures it can affect pipes if they are not deep enough, or when exposed after digging up.

There is a rumour that we may get television in three months' time.

January 23rd 1973

I hadn't been back long before it was time to go out for our annual conference. This year it was held at the Hotel Chantecler in Ste Adèle in the Laurentian Mountains. It was right on the ski slope so as we had two hours for lunch every day, I went skiing instead. Some of us went night skiing at Mont Gabriel as well. The social life in the evenings was good and we danced nearly every night.

Since Judy Hill's death (the English nurse who was killed in a small plane), we have had a lot of new regulations on air safety. We are supposed to check that the pilots are sober, (joke!) and that their radio equipment and alarm beeps are in working order before boarding. The other day, after the conference, leaving Timmins, we jokingly asked the pilot if he was SURE his radio and beeps were working. Half an hour out of Timmins the plane turned back to Timmins as all the alarm lights came on and the radio was out of order. We couldn't help laughing because the pilot said it was OK before we started asking questions! An hour later we set off again with no mishaps.

I have bought 18 new records this month: *Bach's Brandenburg concertos*, *Play Bach* (jazz), Mozart's horn concertos, Elgar's *Pomp and Circumstance* marches, Vivaldi's Four Seasons, a collection of Canadian folk songs and a George Brassens record.

February 5th 1973

Things are pretty busy here. On 29th January Dr Delva arrived to do a paediatric survey so we have been examining children non-stop. After nine days, he hopes to have examined 400 children. I must say, I am very pleased with the way it is going, everyone is turning up at the appointed time and we are doing well. The interpreter goes out with the list and calls the people for the next day. Dr Delva trained in London and lived most of his life in England but his parents were Belgian. He and his wife and four children are now living in Sherbrook and are happy in Canada.

Last weekend I went for a long walk with Carol, Denise and their little girl, Julie (on a sled), such a nice French Canadian family. We walked across to the other side of the river. The Canso that crashed is another hour further on and I would like to go and see that before the ice melts.

February 20th 1973

Dr Delva was really good fun to work with and we saw 425 children in eight days. We worked really hard, some evenings and Saturday too, it was very satisfying.

I have been curling for the first and probably last time in my life! One night last week Carol asked me if I could replace him as he couldn't go. It didn't matter that I had never done it before. I was the only woman there and I was flat on my face, exhausted trying to push the thing. All evening I only got it over the red line once. Quite an experience but it's not for me.

A Cree man went south for an appendicectomy a few weeks ago and came back with an infected wound. I tried a variety of antibiotics for several weeks, to no avail. His wife came to ask me if she could try a traditional Labrador Tea infusion to put on his wound. As I had tried everything I could, there was nothing to lose. After 10 days of Labrador Tea, his wound is now perfectly healed!

March 1st 1973

I have been fairly busy lately and seem to have had a lot of interrupted nights. As I am on my own at night, I get all the night calls; mostly minor things but it still means interrupted sleep. Last Thursday I was called at midnight for a white man whose clothes had caught fire in the garage. His hand was badly burned but he was lucky not to have been more seriously injured. Then, the same night, I was called at 4.30 a.m. for a woman who told me she was in labour. I was so tired, I said rather crossly to her, "You can't be, you're not due yet!" I knew there would be no more sleep for a couple of nights. I felt guilty because she really was in labour. It was a breech delivery (my second breech!) at 7.10 a.m. Officially she should have gone to hospital but she was a bit premature. The delivery went well anyway. Then, a midwife's nightmare, she had an eclamptic fit. Despite all my midwifery experience, it was the first time I had had a case of eclampsia. (The mother's blood pressure goes dangerously high) She only had one fit but her blood pressure wouldn't go down despite sedation. I kept her with me all weekend and escorted her out on a stretcher to Moose Factory hospital on Monday. It was 50 below that day and we sat in the plane for an hour before take-off. I thought my feet would never come round again. When we finally arrived at the hospital I was relieved to pass my patient over to the experts. I spent the night there so was able to have a rest myself.

Moose Factory hospital is on an island but planes land at Moosonee about two miles away, on the mainland. In the winter the 'road' across the ice is even given a layer of gravel, so you don't even know you are crossing a river. In the summer of course, the only way across is by boat. Someone suggested that the song *'Sailing down the River'* should be called 'Driving down the River'.

The weather is clear and sunny most of the time and the evenings are getting longer. I have been trying more photos of the Aurora Borealis.

The mail has been very spasmodic lately. It was much more reliable when Austin Airways had the mail contract because we always have at least one Austin Airways plane a week whereas Nordair, who now have the contract, can miss one or two weeks.

CHAPTER 12
TB INTERLUDE

March 14th 1973
THE ROYAL EDWARD CHEST HOSPITAL MONTREAL

I had a little trip out to the bush last week. A Cree Indian man walked 45 miles in 12 hours to tell me that his wife was very sick so I chartered a plane (Austin Airways DC3) to bring her out. We landed on a nearby lake and the man took me to their tent. By the time we got there his wife Alice was packing up their belongings, the children were all dressed and ready to leave. It seems this was a ruse to get a free trip back to Great Whale. This sort of thing happens periodically and I had to be very firm and say I had come to fetch Alice and Alice ONLY. They weren't very happy. Alice was ill but certainly not dangerously so. This was a difficult situation.

I do have some varied experiences! I am now a patient in Montreal Chest hospital.

On Sunday, after church, Connie came back to the nursing station with me and hung around, so we had coffee. She obviously had something on her mind as she usually goes straight home after church. I wondered what it was. Eventually she told me she had picked up a telegram on Friday to say that I had to go out on the next plane for TB investigations. She didn't want to ruin my weekend by telling me on Friday. In actual fact I was secretly relieved and wondered if six weeks sleep would be long enough for me. I didn't say this of course and Connie was surprised I was so calm. I have been extremely tired lately but put it down to all the night calls.

I left Great Whale yesterday for Montreal. Both Pam and Dr Mally, our TB consultant, were there to meet me at the airport which was nice. We all went out to dinner before coming to the hospital. It seems that one of the sputum specimens I sent out in November (after our housekeeper Winnie's diagnosis) was positive. So now I will have to have more tests and X-rays which will take eight weeks before all the results are back. I may start TB medication soon, depending on results. The first person I met here was Lally Yuyusi from Sugluk! There are a couple of Eskimos here from Clyde River too. I am sharing a room with Lally and a French Canadian woman.

March 25th 1973
THE ROYAL EDWARD CHEST HOSPITAL

This is a very friendly little hospital. I have now been here 12 days and am having a wonderful rest. It's like a holiday. As all my tests so far have been negative, they are wondering if it was a laboratory error but I still have to wait another six weeks before the final cultures come back before I am allowed back to work. I shall probably be sent up to the TB sanatorium in the Laurentian Mountains in the meantime.

It is an interesting experience for me. We all talk 'TB' all the time: we compare skin tests, talk about the tests we had today, who is going home, what did the doctor say? How big is your cavity? What drugs are you taking? etc.. Actually, it is pretty hard on people having to leave their families for six weeks or more. Adults are allowed to visit but not children. At least it is an improvement on the old days, when people were in TB sanatoria for years and often never came out.

March 29th 1973
LAURENTIAN CHEST HOSPITAL STE AGATHE.

So here I am in the sanatorium! On Tuesday I came in a taxi with Flor, a Phillipino girl. The taxi driver was very chatty. He has been doing trips between the two hospitals for 10 years, so has seen a few changes. 10 years ago sanatoria were always full. Here there were originally three three-storey buildings. One burned down and another was pulled down, leaving just one of which only two floors are now used. There are 22 patients on the women's floor and 32 on the men's floor.

We arrived at 12 p.m. just in time for lunch. Our suitcases went up ahead of us and while we were still in the admissions office, a group of Eskimos came down to see the new admissions. They immediately took Flor to be Eskimo, with her Chinese features, which was interesting. They bombarded her with questions before they realised she was not Eskimo! Flor, of course, wondered what was going on. Rebecca, a lovely Eskimo woman from POV, took me on a tour of the hospital. In the lift, we met the doctor who asked me, "Are you the one here under false pretences?" I must say, I do feel a bit of a fraud.

Flor and I each have single rooms next door to each other. There are six or seven Eskimos, from POV, Clyde River, Frobisher Bay and Lally from Sugluk. Most of the white patients seem to be middle-aged or elderly. Flor and I, both the same age, are the youngest here.

The food is good; we have breakfast at 8 a.m., lunch at 12, supper at 5 and at 7.30 they bring out a trolley with tea, bread and jam and cereals. I suppose the idea is to fatten us up. I have lost a lot of weight these past few weeks too.

We have films twice a week, a canteen, library with records as well as books, games and jig-saw puzzles. There are three or four different televisions too. It is rather like being on a ship in a way but by the end of six weeks I'll probably be glad to disembark. I'm sleeping 11 to 18 hours a day which is wonderful. We are allowed to have our beds out on the balcony during the day but not at night as they say it is too cold. There is still quite a lot of snow around. I am too hot at night in my room so have permission to sleep next to the open French windows in an empty ward at night. The closest I can get to being outside! I am used to sleeping in sub-zero temperatures with my window open now. I can't sleep in the heat.

We have a direct line to Montreal here but as it has to be shared by the whole hospital I don't suppose I shall phone much.

There are different categories of patients with their own rules and privileges. (I am in category C and taking advantage of all rest periods).

LIST OF RULES:

CATEGORY A: Acute toxic conditions. Complete bed rest. No telephone calls. Bed baths.

CATEGORY B: Haemorrhage and/or toxic cases. Bed rest, bed baths, to bathroom in wheelchair with special permission. Meals in bed, no telephone calls, No visiting in other patient rooms.

CATEGORY C: For non-toxic regular new patients. Full bathroom privileges. Up for meals, may be up between rest periods. May visit library, O.T. and attend movies. May watch TV after cure hours. May visit rooms of patients of the same sex. Sunday passes with special permission.

CATEGORY D: Full bathroom privileges, make and change own bed, ground passes between 10.30 and 12 Noon and 3.30 and 5.30 p.m. Sunday pass 4 hours, with permission.

REST PERIODS:

9.00 - 10.30: Patients in Categories A, B, and C must be in bed but may read or write. No TV or radios. Category D patients may visit library, canteen or O.T. but be in bed if they stay in their rooms, so as not to disturb others.

1 p.m. - 3 p.m.: ALL patients must be in bed and try to rest. No TV or radios.

6 p.m. - 7 p.m.: ALL patients must be on their beds, TV and radios allowed but not too loud.

ALL patients should prepare for bed by 10.15 p.m. Lights out, TV and radios off 10.45.

Yesterday I had my first 'shopping pass' and walked down to the village. My first time out for two weeks. It felt quite strange.

April 9th 1973

Time is not dragging at all as I thought it would. As well as continuing to sleep through all the rest periods (and I'm now in Category D), I am reading a lot (detective stories, which make good 'holiday reading') and letter writing. Flor and I play Scrabble every day, she is very good. I have had quite a few visitors from the office and Mlle Laurin has even been up herself. That was an unexpected surprise. I am trying to work on my Inuktituk with the Eskimos here. There are eight in all at the moment. Other nationalities include: Chinese, Indian, Jamaican, Spanish and a few British. White Canadians are in the minority. I usually go out for a bit in the afternoon; the weather has turned sunny now. Flor is not allowed out yet.

April 16th 1973

I have had some more tests and am booked for a bronchoscopy on May 2nd. I'm dreading that.

The Eskimos have all been rather homesick lately with lots of tears. I have been trying to give what comfort I can, with my limited Inuktituk. Yesterday, as one of the nurses was off sick and the other had to cover both floors, I took all the temperatures on this floor. It was nice to be helping for a change. Flor and I continue to play two or three games of Scrabble a day and read a lot.

TB Sanatorium: Rebecca (left) and Lally

April 21st 1973

Our snow is almost gone now and I am getting a sun tan lying on my bed out on the balcony. What luxury!

Alice came up with a friend of hers on Thursday and we drove out into the country to bask in the sun. We had dinner in Ste Adèle before coming back here. That was a nice break. I also had a brief visit from Father Verspeek, who had been in hospital himself in Montreal. He is staying in a monastery there while waiting to go back to Sugluk. It was lovely to see him too.

My bronchoscopy will now be on the 9th May. (Another week's grace!)

When I first arrived here I was quite overawed, even as a nurse, by all the tests I had to have. I wondered what it must be like for the Eskimos who hadn't even ever seen a flush toilet. I decided to make a film-strip project for Eskimos, on what it is like to go to hospital. I am calling it 'Rebecca Goes to Hospital' and Rebecca, who comes from POV, is my main star. We have had great fun doing it and all the staff have been very helpful. I had Rebecca dressed in her coat with her suitcase 'arriving' at the hospital, going for X-rays, blood tests, having her blood pressure taken, photos of the doctor's round, meal times and nurses' drug rounds etc. as well as what bathrooms and flush toilets look like. I have taken 45 slides altogether and they have all come out well.

On Easter Monday Huguette (one of the nurses from the Montreal office who lives in Ste Agathe), came to visit me and take me out. We hired bikes and cycled round the lake (without doctor's permission!) It was a gorgeous day, perfect for cycling.

May 1st 1973

I am very relieved. They no longer feel it is necessary for me to have a bronchoscopy! Tomorrow I am returning to The Royal Edward hospital. After this wonderful 'holiday in the sun' I shall be sorry to leave. I shall also miss the other patients, particularly Flor but we will stay in touch.

May 3rd 1973
ROYAL EDWARD HOSPITAL   MONTREAL

Here I am back in the Royal Edward again. They want to do some more tests to find out why I am still running a temperature, have lost more weight and there is no sign of TB.

May 10th 1973
ROYAL EDWARD HOSPITAL

After all the tests it seems I might have had hepatitis but it will remain a mystery. I have been advised not to drink alcohol for three months. I'm having some convalescence before going back to Great Whale.

May 31st 1973
MONTREAL

Mlle Laurin and Dr Mally have decided that I should now work somewhere where I would be doing just public health nursing, not dealing with sick people and where I can use my newly acquired diploma to better effect. They want me to go to Fort George where I will be working with Ursula. I am really excited about this and I think the change will be good for me. Another new experience!

I spent a week with Marianne and Manou, friends from Switzerland who are now living in Quebec. They have three little boys aged eight months, two years and three years. I was to sleep downstairs on their sofa but found I couldn't sleep with the central heating. I didn't know what to do until I hit on the idea of taking the cushions out to the porch. There was snow outside and no heating in the porch so it was perfect. Marianne was amazed to find me out there in the morning! I also had a few days here in Montreal before going back to Great Whale. I'm looking forward to going back after all this time. Mlle Laurin was very impressed by my film strip and she suggested that I start the film with Rebecca arriving at Montreal airport. As I wasn't doing anything for a few days I was left to organise this. I phoned the sanatorium and Rebecca was put in the hospital taxi, wearing her winter coat and carrying her suitcase (as in the original slide). I picked her up at the Royal Edward and together with Eva, the Eskimo interpreter from the office, as well as the use of the government car for the morning, we set off for the airport. Poor Rebecca, in her winter coat! We all had a marvellous time photographing Rebecca's arrival at the airport, being met by Eva, collecting her suitcase off the carousel and put into the taxi for Ste Agathe. After this, I took Rebecca out to lunch and took her back to Ste Agathe on the bus in the afternoon. She was so excited and kept telling me how happy she was and thanking me. I told her I was very happy too. She had her eyes wide open all the time and must have seen hundreds of things she had never seen before. It would also have been her first time in a bus.

Tomorrow I leave for Great Whale.

June 6th 1973
GREAT WHALE RIVER

On June 1st, I left Montreal to get the 10.30 flight back here and had to escort nine-year-old Bobby who lives in Sugluk. We were told the plane was delayed until 2 p.m. so I took Bobby for some breakfast as he had left in too much of a hurry and was hungry. At 1 p.m. we were told that the plane was cancelled. Bobby was collected by Eva and I went to Pam's for the night. The next day the plane took off at 10.30 but we had to stop in Val d'Or for about one and a half hours, waiting for Great Whale's weather which was apparently 'not good'. There was thick fog over Great Whale and we circled round for 20 minutes. I thought we would be returning to Montreal but the pilot landed WITH the wind. What a bump!

It was wonderful to be back again after almost three months. I went to supper with Denise and Carol and afterwards we went to a party at the bar, (Coke only for me but that didn't detract from my enjoyment at all) which was lovely. I went to bed at 2 a.m. and was woken at 5.15 a.m. to go and bring an emergency out of POV. We now have a little Twin Otter Plane based here. As it doesn't need as much ice to land as a DC3, it can land on thinner ice during some of the break-up. We left at 6 a.m. arriving in POV at 9 o'clock. The patient was a 14-year-old boy who had accidentally shot himself in the shoulder. He was conscious, on a stretcher. We stopped in Port Harrison to re-fuel and Denise came out to the plane for a chat which was nice. We arrived in Fort George about 2 p.m. and the boy was admitted to the hospital. As that plane wasn't returning to Great Whale I stayed the night with Ursula at the health centre. She had invited some friends around and cooked goose which was delicious.

I was supposed to be returning to Great Whale with the DC3 the next day but there were already too many passengers and I couldn't get on. I didn't mind having another day in Fort George.

As I am going to be working in Fort George from the end of the month, it was really good to start getting to know people. Everyone seems very friendly. It was like a summer's afternoon with temperatures in the 70s. Some of the white people, including myself, were invited to a friend's for charcoal steaks, which were cooked and eaten outside. Later I was invited to the rectory for coffee while Ursula was out.

I am looking forward to working there with Ursula. We immediately got on when we first met. The health centre is very homely and the living room has a fireplace. Plenty of trees here, for firewood. As Ursula lives with her husband Guy, in a teacher's house, I shall be living on my own in the nurse's accommodation. Ursula and I will be doing public health nursing only as the hospital deals with sick people so there are no night calls for us.

The following day, there was no plane so I had another day off. Guy and Ursula have just acquired a month-old St Bernard puppy, Sherry. She is the cutest thing, really comical. She weighs six pounds at the moment but in the next two years her adult weight will reach about 200 pounds. That evening we went to the school residence where Cree Indian children from Paint Hills and

Rupert's House, both in the James Bay area, board. They have films there twice a week and we watched a western.

The Cree Indians in Fort George seem to live a much more traditional life than those in Great Whale. In Fort George there are about 1600 Cree Indians and a small group of about 50 Eskimos.

The next morning we got up at 5 a.m. as there was to be a Cree 'Initiation' ceremony for all babies who had been born since last spring, ages ranging from 12 to 18 months-old. This was to celebrate the babies' first symbolic steps in life. The floor of the teepee was covered with fresh spruce branches and a fire was lit. The babies were dressed in new white parkas, the boys with a hood and the girls each wore a head scarf. They all wore new kamiks, the boys each carried a little wooden gun and a harpoon and the girls carried a little wooden axe and wore a bag containing flour and sugar round their necks. (Symbolising their male and female roles). Once everyone was assembled the babies were walked around the inside of the teepee on the clean branches, then all round the outside of it. Back inside, the chief, sitting on a bearskin, talked and prayed at length in Cree. Finally the babies were passed around everyone in the teepee to be kissed. The ceremony finished about 6.45. Luckily, I never go anywhere without my camera. I got the plane back to Great Whale, arriving about 12 p.m.

June 16th 1973

Rebecca has been discharged from the TB Sanatorium and she came through Great Whale on her way back to POV. I managed to take photos of her getting out of the Nordair Jet and getting into the Twin Otter. She looked so happy to be going home again. Now I have the complete slide set and I am going to start on the sound track.

I am packing up my things again and looking forward to moving to Fort George. I should be leaving on 4th July, after Connie gets back from her holiday.

Fort George: Spring ceremony, Cree baby girl (top), Cree baby boy (bottom)

CHAPTER 13
FORT GEORGE

July 12th 1973
FORT GEORGE

A week ago I left Great Whale to come here. It was a busy final week in Great Whale, with Connie away on holiday and I had to send Christine, the new nurse, out on escort with a stretcher case.

It was an hour's flight from Great Whale to Fort George with Austin Airways' DC3. This is the most gorgeous place I have lived in yet. The health centre was built in 1942 (very old by Canadian standards). I have a big living room with a fireplace, bedroom, bathroom and kitchen. There is another bathroom and bedroom on the other side, with the clinic. There are windows on all sides with a beautiful view over the river. There is much more vegetation here; trees, shrubs, grass and flowers. I even have grass and trees in my garden though a lot of the village is sand. Great Whale was sandy but here it is even more so. Right behind my house there are two beautiful walks along the river, one along the beach and the other higher up. Ursula and I went for a walk at the weekend with Sherry, their adorable St Bernard puppy. She is now two and a half months old and weighs 24lbs.

July 22nd 1973
STE AGATHE

Here I am in the Laurentians again! I had to go to Montreal for my check-up and it took 12 hours to get there. Although Fort George is further south, on the James Bay, it is less accessible than Great Whale. No planes fly direct from Fort George to Montreal. Austin Airways fly three times a week from here to Timmins, Nordair flies three times a week to Val d'Or and Fecteau flies four times a week to Val d'Or, from where there are direct flights to Montreal.

I left Fort George with a Fecteau DC3 at 12 p.m. on Thursday. There were just two of us flying out, myself and Julie, a hospital secretary going out on holiday. Val d'Or was closed-in because of fog so we flew on to Amos which was also fogged-in. We finally landed in Matagami. We were enquiring about bus services to Val d'Or when the pilot of a little Twin Engine Islander offered to fly us there as he was going anyway. 45 minutes later we were in Val d'Or but just missed the Montreal flight by minutes. The next one was at 9.30 p.m., six hours away. There is nothing to do at the airport so Julie and I went into town and looked round the shops. People were very friendly and we chatted to shopkeepers. Val d'Or is a gold mining town, hence the name. Back at the airport, I bumped into Noella Roussel who is a nursing officer in this area returning to the Montreal office. She invited me to spend the night with her as Pam was away. The next day, I went to the Royal Edward hospital for my check-up. After waiting two hours, the doctor told me I looked fine and said if I felt fine he could close my file. I could have WRITTEN to tell him that! I was a bit fed-up, having come all that way, especially as none of my friends in Montreal were home.

The prospect of a weekend in Montreal, alone, in the heat of the summer was not appealing so I phoned Rita in Ste Agathe who invited me for the weekend. Rita was the nurse in charge on my ward at the sanatorium and we had become friends. She had been very good to me. I phoned Huguette at the office to see whether she was going home that weekend to Ste Agathe and she was so gave me a lift.

On the Saturday Rita was giving a dinner party and Raymond, a famous French Canadian artist, was invited, as he was holding an exhibition in Ste Agathe that weekend. 20 years ago, Rita nursed him in the sanatorium, where he was admitted at the age of 18, dying of TB. He had been given three months to live so had given all his possessions away, including all his painting materials and was resigned to ending his days in the sanatorium. Three months later, Rita told me, he started showing a lot of interest in the ward maids so they decided he had better have some occupational therapy and he started painting again. 18 months later he was discharged. He has always loved this area and often comes back to paint and to visit Rita and her family. Monique, another ex-patient, was at the party with a friend. She had been in the Sanatorium at the same time as Raymond but was there for five years. After dinner, we all went to the exhibition and I bought my first oil painting ($225). 'Les Nénuphars' (Water lilies), so I'm thrilled with that. Raymond told me that grey and ochre, which are the main colours, are his favourite colours. He told me I had picked a good example of his work.

This morning Monique invited us all to a fantastic champagne breakfast (I am now allowed to drink a little) at their wonderful old farmhouse which they are still renovating after four years. So, after all, it has been a marvellous weekend! I have to go to the office tomorrow and hope to fly back to Fort George on Tuesday.

July 29th 1973
FORT GEORGE.

I had another 12½ hour trip back to Fort George! I left the Montreal hotel at 6.45 a.m. for the flight to Matagami, arriving at 10 a.m. Nordair was supposed to leave at 11.30 but the pilot went off on another trip first. Matagami airport is a wooden hut on the airstrip, in the middle of nowhere. Passengers sat around in sweltering heat with flies buzzing around, for seven hours, until 5 o'clock. I was beginning to feel quite ill. We were given sandwiches and a cold drink in cardboard boxes, which we ate on our knees. Eventually Fecteau's DC3 took us back as Nordair's plane had developed mechanical problems so I was finally home at 7.15 p.m. I have since learned that Matagami was the hottest place in Canada that day, with temperatures up to 105 degrees. No wonder I was feeling ill.

I am now on my own in Fort George as Ursula and Guy (and Sherry) are on holiday for six weeks.

August 8th 1973

This summer continues to be very hot, the hottest people remember. A pity the mosquitoes are so bad. Yesterday some of us went fishing; it is a relief to get out on the water, away from the worst of the bugs. We lit a fire at midday and roasted sausages and marshmallows. We stayed out till 6 p.m.

Workwise, as well as baby clinics, preschool clinics, antenatal clinics, TB clinics, school health teaching and visiting the elderly and infirm, there are a few extra duties such as meeting patients from Paint Hills, Eastmain and Rupert's House (the three other villages on the James Bay), who are in transit to Montreal. So I go out to meet the little float planes and make sure the patients are found accommodation if necessary and get them on to the next Montreal plane. Unfortunately the Nordair flight leaves for Montreal (via Val d'Or) at 7 a.m. which means getting up very early to see them off. There is a lot of paper work so I am deep in files again. Elizabeth is our Cree community health worker who has had some basic health training and works with us liaising between us and the Cree population. She goes out to encourage mothers to bring their babies to clinics etc..

There is a helicopter based here at the moment, working with a hydrographic team determining the depth of the water around here. Don, the pilot, offered to take me for a ride one evening. The views were lovely. Suddenly he landed in a very remote area and started making advances to me. I definitely did not want this and made it clear. Luckily, he got the message and we returned to the village. For a moment I was a bit scared as we were in the middle of nowhere at the time. Anyway, no harm was done. I didn't anticipate that! It is wonderful to be able to go out in the evenings and at weekends, without the fear of being called for an emergency. And - to sleep all night!

August 16th 1973

After quite a drought we have had some rain twice this week but the heat continues. There have been two forest fires near here, one between here and Great Whale and one about 60 miles east of here at LG2. (One of the James Bay Project camps, explained below). The fire jumped the river at LG2 and everyone there had to be evacuated. It was heading here quite fast, at about five miles an hour at one stage. They were trying to fight it with helicopters but it was futile. The first day, it began to get dark, rather like an eclipse; the sky was completely clouded over and the village enveloped in smoke. We had visions of our being evacuated and I started wondering how I would start packing up, what would have priority. I decided I would pack all the files and papers into the fridge and freezer as there was a chance they would be saved from the fire inside solid metal. Anyway, we had some rain a couple of days later and the wind changed direction. I don't know if the fire has burned out now, I haven't heard.

LG2 is one of the camps connected with the James Bay Project. The project is a big scandal. Americans (I think) and the Quebec government started the project about a year ago. The river La Grande is supposed to be one of the biggest in Canada and has fantastic power potential. There is going to be massive flooding, machinery will drive away animals and the river is being polluted. It has caused great upset because it is seriously interfering with the lives of the James Bay Indians. Naturally, the Indians have not been consulted. They are up in arms about it and are trying to sue the project but no-one knows how successful they will be. There are about six camps, LG1 to 6, and hundreds of men involved. These men are also 'importing' drugs and this is another new problem.

About four or five years ago the Cree Indians here didn't even have alcohol. Times are changing.

Fruit is terrific this year; Margaret (my cleaning lady) brought me a basin of blue berries and I went out with Cliff and Myra who run the Hudson's Bay store, to pick wild raspberries and redcurrants. I made two pounds of redcurrant jelly which is absolutely delicious with a wild flavour. I don't want it to finish!

August 22nd 1973

Dr Simard came on Friday for a business lunch here with Dr Dumont from the hospital. Priscille, the zone nursing officer from Montreal also came and stayed the weekend with me which was nice. We were both invited to Cliff and Myra's for barbecued T-Bone steaks on Sunday.

It is just starting to get a bit chilly and I have had the furnace on all day today. It is VERY noisy so I shall wait until it gets really cold before I leave it on at night.

August 29th 1973

The other day, I had just got home after my afternoon home visiting when I had a phone call from Christine saying she was stranded here at the airport with another nurse, on her way back to Great Whale with eight patients. Great Whale weather was bad and they would have to spend the night here. I went down to pick them up, find homes for the eight patients and then return for the luggage. While I was at the airport, Walter the Austin Airways agent, asked me if I had seen a little boy who came down from POV on the Canso. I said I hadn't seen him and Walter told me that Cliff had taken him to the health centre. I said I would no doubt find him when I went back. However, no sign of a little boy when I did get home and I asked Margaret if she had seen him. Apparently, Cliff had given this frightened and crying six-year-old over to Margaret to look after and shortly after Margaret heard me come in and go straight out again she presumed I had taken the child with me as he had disappeared. I phoned the police and they went to look for the child. He was soon found, very frightened and crying and I found a family to look after him. I then set to to find some food for supper for three.

Christine managed to get away with half her patients on the plane the next day and Paulette, the other nurse, stayed another night and left this afternoon. So what with my busy clinics and trying to run a 'travel agency' it has been very hectic. It will be wonderful to have Ursula back again next week after seven weeks on my own.

September 10th 1973

Ursula came back on Friday and it was lovely to see her again. Sherry has almost tripled her weight in those seven weeks and now weighs 60lbs. A mere four-month-old pup!

I have been working hard on the sound track to my film-strip. I can only do it at night when it is quiet because of the tape recorder. I have recorded the background music and now have to superimpose my voice with a second tape recorder. I also needed some kind of signal so that the person who is showing the film knows when to change the slide so I have a 'bell' which I devised by hitting a glass with a knife approximately every ten seconds. Every time I make a mistake, I have to start again so it has taken me many hours to synchronise the sound track. The photography was the easy bit. I also had to do it in French which has made the timing difficult because it often takes longer to say something in French so 10 seconds is not always long enough.

We now seem to be having a 'rainy season'. Elizabeth, our community health worker and I were out visiting with the jeep the other day in the rain and it got stuck deep in the sand. We had to be pulled out by stronger vehicles.

September 26th 1973

The post office has been out of action for about 10 days. The postmaster left with a couple of days' notice and they had to find a new one. Another Fort George Indian has taken over but he had to wait for the Val d'Or postmaster to come up and show him the ropes. In the meantime Austin Airways office has piled higher and higher with mail. It will still be a few days before we get back to normal. I have been taking advantage of anyone going south to post my letters.

My film-strip is almost finished. Soundtracks are completed in English and French and I managed to find a Cree girl to do it in Cree. It took us about three hours. She was terrific as each time something went wrong we had to start again but she was very patient. The hours it has taken for this 12 minute film-strip! I am going to ask Eva, our Eskimo interpreter in Montreal, to do it in Eskimo.

We have lots of time to do home visits here and it is lovely to be out amongst the people in the village. The Indians here put their babies in hammocks to sleep and the mother or grandmother will sit and rock the hammock. One day I went into a house and heard a woman singing in Cree. To my surprise, no-one was home except the baby in the hammock with a tape recorder nearby. The mother had recorded herself singing. Another day I saw an old man walking with the aid of a broom handle, accompanied by his two-year-old grandchild with nothing on but a T-shirt and rubber boots on the wrong feet. Pity I didn't have my camera. Older children seem to be spending all their time shooting at birds with slingshots. They can be seen crouching and creeping up on the birds. I have spotted them in my garden hiding in the bushes. It used to upset me to see this until I realised that children have to start somewhere with their hunting skills. There also seem to be quite a few broken windows as a result.

October 7th 1973

We are having some nice sunny autumn weather and Ursula and I take Sherry (who now weighs 77lbs) for long walks along the beach. This afternoon we saw a musk rat so Sherry and Bobo (another little dog) chased it and barked at it. The musk rat would run away when chased then suddenly would turn back without warning and run towards the predator. Ursula put sherry on the lead as she was worried about rabies and I managed to approach the musk rat with my camera. I took one photo and got closer for another when suddenly it made a run for me! I ran for my life leaving one of my boots behind in the mud. We really laughed!

October 22nd 1973

I have just spent five days in Montreal, all expenses paid, so that I could finish my film-strip in Eskimo. Sarah May, the other Eskimo interpreter with Eva, in the office, did the script. Poor girl! She almost lost her voice by the end of the recording session. Sarah is Johnny May's sister. He is still a pilot in the Fort Chimo area. Everyone in the office is very impressed by the film strip; I gave them all a showing. Mlle Laurin wants to make copies of it so that all the health centres in the Quebec region can have a copy. She has asked me to do it in Montagnais, another Indian language. I met the Montagnais interpreter Fernande, who speaks French but not English, explained what we would be doing and later in the afternoon we spent over three hours recording. She was rather tired at the end. So *'Rebecca Goes to Hospital'* is now in five languages! I will be able to keep the original and the office is going to pay for the copying. It will have to be sent away to Kodak.

All the slides I took of the northern lights one night last month have come out well. They were particularly spectacular that night. Many people said they had never seen such fantastic lights. I certainly hadn't.

October 30th 1973

The clocks changed this weekend but quite a few of us didn't realise until the Monday. Not that it mattered much on Sunday anyway.

Two maintenance men from the Montreal office were planning to spend the freeze-up in Paint Hills and ordered 11 boxes of food which were sent to me to send on. It took me hours to unpack all the food and put it in the fridge then a couple of days later, pack it all up again to put on the plane. Then the plane, which was the last before the freeze-up, was cancelled so I 'inherited' all that food and had to unpack it again! I have been inviting people for meals to help eat it all and given some away as I don't have room to store it all. On Sunday we had an 'all fruit' breakfast.

November 11th 1973

We have at last got some snow, which only started settling a few days ago. It is very late this year.

Fort George: Cree baby in hammock

November 28th 1973

I had two birthday celebrations this year! Cliff and Myra invited me for one and Ursula and Guy, the other.

The mail is still in chaos, the new postmaster can hardly cope with it. There is apparently a backlog in Moosonee, so with Christmas approaching, things are very slow. Myra is going to Montreal tomorrow so I will give her my mail to post there.

December 21st 1973

Last weekend Guy and Ursula and I (and Sherry of course) went across the river with two ski-doos, to fetch Christmas trees. It was a beautiful day and we walked around on snow shoes. Sherry had a marvellous time, sinking deep at every step. She now weighs about 125lbs.

Guy and Ursula are going to have Christmas dinner with me. It will be very cosy with the fire. It will be the first time I have ever cooked Christmas dinner.

Ursula and I have decided to hold a Christmas party for all the old people, probably about 40, on January 3rd. Elizabeth is going to cook some geese and Ursula and I will make cakes and biscuits etc.. It will be good for the people to get together.

It has been getting progressively colder this week and we had a big storm lasting a couple of days. This house is very draughty and the furnace has never been very effective but I was told I would have to wait until January to get it repaired. On Wednesday the wind was howling through the front door and the temperature inside was only 60 degrees. I phoned Ursula to advise her to stay at home while I spent the morning borrowing heaters and moving everything for the clinic downstairs to the basement where it was a bit warmer. By the afternoon, with an extra heater and the oven on, it was warm enough for the baby clinic. I have been very glad of my fire in the evenings. Guy came over after the baby clinic and was quite shocked by how cold it was. He went to look at the furnace and discovered the cause of the problem: a couple of turns with a screwdriver was all it took, the thermostat was still on its summer setting! So now I know what to do in future. And to think I was just going to put up with it until January.

The washing machine has now broken down. It goes through the washing cycle but won't empty the water out. The plumber has looked at it but says the problem is probably electrical and there is no electrician here at the moment. I have to empty the machine with a saucepan but at least it does the washing.

CHAPTER 14
FORT GEORGE AND RUPERT'S HOUSE
1974

January 6th 1974
FORT GEORGE

On Thursday Ursula, Elizabeth and I gave our party for the over 65s. 50 people came and they all enjoyed themselves. Some of them hadn't seen each other for years.

We have been out across the river ski-dooing and snow-shoeing quite a lot over Christmas. I have bought some snow shoes, locally made, as they are really necessary in deep snow. It is getting colder, down to about 40 below and will get even colder from now on.

January 13th 1974

The telephones have been very temperamental since New Year's Eve. It is a tradition here, at midnight on New Year's Eve, for the Indians to fire a rifle into the air and somebody inadvertently shot through the main telephone cable! We had no phones at all for a few days. At the moment we never know whether they will work or not.

I'm getting excited about going home now. Only just over a month until February 21st when I leave here.

Rupert's House: village (top), single engine Otter
plane (bottom)

January 18th 1974
RUPERT'S HOUSE

On Monday I had a radio call from Montreal to ask me to come here to Rupert's House for two weeks to replace the nurses while they are at the conference. I quickly threw some things together in a suitcase ready to fly that afternoon. The plane was cancelled due to bad weather down the coast. On Tuesday the plane got as far as Moosonee but had to turn back again.

On Wednesday Connie arrived in Fort George in a real state as, on her way back to Great Whale after escorting a patient to Moose Factory Hospital, the pilot was denied entry as Great Whale was in quarantine for smallpox! Connie was understandably very worried as her husband Steve and baby Brian were at home there. As I was leaving for Rupert's House I wondered what would happen if the whole coast were closed, which naturally it would be if smallpox were confirmed. I could be in Rupert's House until the summer. What a disaster a smallpox epidemic would be!

I eventually left Fort George on the Wednesday at 2 p.m. in a single engine Otter on skis. We stopped at Paint Hills and Eastmain arriving in Rupert's House about 4.30. None of these three villages on the James Bay has an airstrip so they are all affected by the freeze-up. The freeze-up only lasts about eight weeks in this area unlike Sugluk where it was three months.

The plane landed on the river, several miles from the village and an Indian was there to meet me with his ski-doo to take me to the nursing station. The nurses had already left for the conference. Bella, the Cree interpreter and community health worker was waiting for me and showed me round the nursing station. It is only two years old, rather like a chalet. It seems very modern compared to most I have seen.

Rupert's House village is only about the same size as Sugluk but with a population of about 500 to 800 Cree Indians, depending on how many are in the bush. The place is quite overcrowded as there aren't enough houses for everyone. Many are living in tents in the village and there are usually about 300 out in the bush. It is a very picturesque little village with wooden shacks. There are beaver skins drying stretched out on frames on poles outside almost every house.

It is quite quiet at the moment as all the normal clinics have been cancelled so I will only have to deal with sick people and emergencies. (I expect there will be some).

Much to my dismay, I seem to have inherited a little ginger kitten which apparently belongs to one of the nurses. He is very naughty and chases things around the desk when I'm trying to write. He is almost house-trained, only one 'accident' so far. I shall have to remember to feed him. No-one mentioned a kitten.

This is a beautiful house, the nurses' accommodation is upstairs and has a fireplace in the living room. It's very cosy. There are rooms for in-patients at the other end upstairs and the clinic and stock rooms are in the basement.

I nearly locked myself out on my first night here; I went downstairs to shut the kitten in the basement and found that the upstairs door had locked behind me. I had visions of spending the night down there and still being in my nightdress when Bella arrived the next morning. However, I managed to find some keys in a drawer and one of them fitted.

The next day I phoned Montreal, (there are real telephones here), to see what the latest news on the smallpox was. Apparently it turned out to be a severe case of chickenpox so that is a relief.

Yesterday Bella showed me round the village and introduced me to people. There are about 28 white people here. We stopped at the mission for a cup of tea and Father Provenchy invited me to supper. Fortune, one of the teachers, who is French Canadian, lives at the mission. Charlie, a pilot, is also staying there. We had a fantastic meal and pleasant evening.

There are two schools here, federal and provincial; Hudson's Bay store, Roman Catholic mission, Anglican mission and a game warden.

I think the next two weeks will go quickly and then I only have three more weeks in Fort George before I leave the north.

Rupert's House: Cree tent

January 23rd 1974
RUPERT'S HOUSE

I am really enjoying my stay here and although I was disappointed not to be going to the conference, I'm glad now I didn't. I do love these small villages. I have taken lots of photos already. The beaver skins drying add to the atmosphere. Apparently the beaver season is almost finished. Winter skins are much thicker than summer skins so I have bought two, an adult skin for $20 and a baby skin for $5. I had to take them to the game warden to pay the royalty money to register them. I asked if I would have any trouble taking them to England and he gave me an exportation form.

On Saturday morning the kindergarten teacher asked me if she could bring her children on a tour of the nursing station. We divided the children into two groups and Bella took one and I took the other. It was a busy morning and the children loved it. The following Monday they all drew pictures of the experience. The kitten featured in all the pictures! I must say, despite my earlier misgivings, I am now very fond of my little Kitty. The food store obviously impressed the children as well as the fridge and the washing machine. The nurse featured in most pictures and two children could no longer remember if their figures were the nurse or the kitten!

On Saturday afternoon, Father Provenchy invited me to go out to his cabin in the bush. Fortune came too and they lent me a ski-doo. It took about an hour to get out there, through beautiful wooded country. The trees are quite tall here. It was much warmer in the bush than in the village. The snow was beautiful, thick and soft; it looked like a Christmas card. I had meant to bring my snow shoes with me but I forgot them at the last minute with the smallpox scare. Although the snow was deep, it wasn't too heavy and we went for a lovely walk in the woods. It was a gorgeous day. We spent the evening in the cabin, which was really cosy by the time the two stoves and the gas lamps were lit. We had our supper there before coming back to the village. There was a party that night with all the white people so I met most of them. Unfortunately I was called away for a sick baby so didn't go back. I was quite tired after all that ski-dooing and walking. I haven't done that much for a couple of years.

On Sunday evening I went to supper with Ron and Lynn, both teachers, whom I had met in Fort George last June. I took Kitty over as they have a dog and a cat. I thought Kitty might enjoy the outing. It was like a circus with the three of them chasing each other round the house. We played Scrabble after supper.

We had a bad storm on Monday which made walking very difficult, especially as it is so hilly here. There are no vehicles to keep roads open, only ski-doos.

On Tuesday I had a patient I wanted advice about and I thought how wonderful it was going to be having a real phone and to be able to speak directly to a doctor at Moose Factory. The phone was out of order and has been ever since. Never mind.

As I haven't too much to do here in the afternoons I have decided to work on another film-strip. I had already had the idea of doing one on safety in the home so that is what I shall do. We do have some film-strips on home safety but they are made for white people with homes of white people. Indians and Eskimos can't relate to those sort of homes so my idea is to make a film-strip, showing familiar home environments. I am going to call it *'Keep Your Children Safe at Home'*. Bella's little girl Sheila, three years old, will be my main film star. We have already had her doing 'dangerous' things such as playing with knives, a gun, an oil lamp, matches and eating a box of 'pills' (I had to buy several packets of Smarties in order to get all the 'pills' the same colour). I have taken slides of all these events. Sheila is a bright little girl and very cooperative. (I told her the pills were really Smarties).

None of the Indians here have electricity. It is lovely walking through the village in the evening with the smell of wood smoke from every house and the gentle golden glow from oil lamps in the windows. They used to have trees literally on their doorstep years ago but now they have to go further each year to fetch wood.

Rupert's House:
Sheila with grandmother skinning a fox

February 2nd 1974
RUPERT'S HOUSE

I was supposed to have gone back to Fort George yesterday but the two nurses were held up as we had a two day storm here and they didn't arrive till yesterday. Little Kitty has grown since they last saw him. I shall miss him, he is so cute. I shall now be leaving here on Monday, weather permitting, of course.

I have been invited out so much here I have hardly had any time to myself. Yves, the game warden and his wife Francine, a very nice French Canadian couple, invited me to their place one evening for a meal. I think people like to see a new face. I had another evening with Ron and Lynn (teachers) and we had a moose fondue which was absolutely delicious. Two other teachers were there and Fred Ward who works for the National Geographic magazine. He was up here in the summer and spent two weeks living with a family out in the bush. He was to come back in the winter and continue the story of Cree Indians in the bush. Unfortunately that family has since come back to the village so he is looking for another family to take him out to the bush. He showed us some of his slides he took in the summer. He wrote an article on Florida last year and one on Japan which comes out next month. Rupert's House should feature in the autumn.

The Bay ran out of eggs last week so I had to make do with one dozen small eggs for two weeks. I normally eat one dozen large eggs a week. Luckily more came in this week and I have been having eggs for lunch and supper for two days.

My film-strip is going well and I have finished all the photography. Everyone has been very helpful. I have taken photos of babies of different ages inside houses and playing outside. I have one photo of a little girl with her grandmother who is sitting on the floor in their house, skinning a fox. I am now working on the script and hope to start the sound-track when I get back to Fort George.

In the bush near Rupert's House

February 7th 1974
FORT GEORGE

I got back here on Monday, after almost three weeks in Rupert's House. It was a wonderful opportunity to see how the Cree live, in a small village.

February 19th 1974

It is now getting warmer and temperatures are around zero. When it is really cold, i.e. 40 below, the snow makes a terrific resounding noise as you walk over it, it sounds almost hollow. We have got used to walking everywhere as our vehicle has been out of order since before Christmas. I have to stock up the health centre supplies before I leave so the other day I borrowed a child's sledge and headed for the Bay. I had quite a load and at one stage lost it going over a bump. A dog managed to steal some biscuits but nothing more.

We saw some beautiful Northern Lights a few nights ago, colours were varied and they were 'dancing'. It's the first time I have seen them 'dancing'. They only lasted a few minutes and of course would have been impossible to photograph.

I have been working on my film sound track. Choosing the background music was quite difficult. It was a choice between Holst's *'Planets'* or a Liszt Hungarian Rhapsody. Eventually the Hungarian Rhapsody won and it is very suitable. Some of the music coincides perfectly with the slides. There is quite a bit of thundery, loud music, with slow chords (danger) and a good balance of 'tinkly' mischievous music on the high keys. The slides I have got back so far are excellent.

How relative is heat! What a coincidence that my sister Kate and I have both written home recently, commenting on how warm it has been: myself, in the snow in the bush near Rupert's House and Kate in South Africa, with temperatures in the hundreds.

Rupert's House: Beaver skins drying

February 23rd 1974
MONTREAL

I really enjoyed working in Fort George, with Ursula, these past seven months. I shall miss her (and adorable Sherry) but we will stay in touch. Ursula still has family in England so I'm sure she will come and visit me there.

I left Fort George 'on schedule' with Nordair at 1 p.m. on Thursday 21st and arrived at Val d'Or at 2.45 We were told there would be a 15 minute wait-over but not to get out of the plane. A few minutes later they told us we wouldn't be leaving until 4.15 As there is nothing to do at Val d'Or, I decided to phone a travel agency about my flight to California and make reservations for my flight home next month. This would fill in the time nicely while waiting for the plane to continue. I had just got to the reservation stage when someone said the plane was about to take off! I had to thank the travel agency for their help and hang up.

I went to the office yesterday, for the last time and showed them the new film-strip, which is now completed in English and French and there are only 10 more slides still to come. They thought it was excellent and I feel very proud.

This is the end of a very exciting few years in the Canadian

Arctic but I am very happy now, to be going back to Europe. It will be strange to begin with, I expect I shall miss the snow but I am looking forward to seeing my father, my friends and above all, settling down in my little cottage in Somerset. One day I will write a book about my Arctic experiences.

EPILOGUE

It was not easy for me to adapt to civilisation after years in 'the bush'. Readjusting to the climate was also very hard; I missed the cold nights and found it difficult to sleep, especially as I came home to two mild winters and two hot summers, one being the summer of 1975 with its heat-wave and drought. One advantage of the summer though, was the pleasure and freedom of being able to walk around in shorts and a T-shirt, not having to worry about mosquitoes.

After spending so many years in a black and white world, I was very excited by all the colour and took whole reels of film just of green fields with yellow flowers. In the garden my father could not convince me that anything green could be a weed.

For years I was aware of aircraft. In Montreal, just after I left the Arctic, I heard every single plane fly over! Still to this day, night planes sometimes wake me up. A plane in the Arctic invariably meant I had to go out and meet it and at night would always wake me instantly.

I am now very happily retired, living in my little cottage in Somerset.